THE BOOK OF

Light CHINESE *Dishes*

THE   BOOK   OF

Light
CHINESE
Dishes

KATHRYN HAWKINS

Photographed by
SIMON BUTCHER

HPBooks

ANOTHER BEST SELLING VOLUME FROM HP BOOKS

HPBooks
Published by The Berkley Publishing Group
200 Madison Avenue
New York, NY 10016

9 8 7 6 5 4 3 2 1

ISBN 1-55788-206-1

By arrangement with Salamander Books Ltd.

Home Economist: Kathryn Hawkins
Printed in Belgium by Proost International Book Production

CONTENTS

INTRODUCTION

Enjoyed the world over, Chinese cooking is well known for being tasty, quick, full of variety, and above all, usually light and healthful.

With minimum amounts of added fats and oils and maximum use of Chinese seasonings and flavorings, this book shows you how to create a mixture of authentic dishes and healthful alternatives, to make quick and tasty meals that everyone will enjoy.

There are over 100 recipes, for stocks and soups, noodles and rice, poultry and meat, and fish and shellfish, as well as vegetarian dishes, vegetable accompaniments and a desserts section for those of you with a sweet tooth. Each recipe is illustrated in full color, with clear step-by-step instructions, to make light Chinese cooking as quick and easy as possible.

—— LIGHT CHINESE COOKING ——

Cutting down on fat is an important part of the modern-day diet. We are all conscious of the effects of too much fat on the body and how we should keep our intake to moderate levels. Yet this should not affect the quality of the meals we eat. It is still possible to enjoy a wide variety of foods by following these few simple, common-sense guidelines.

HEALTHFUL FOOD PREPARATION

✦ Always choose fresh, lean cuts of meat, poultry and fish. Look for meat with firm flesh, with as few streaks of fat as possible.

✦ Lean meat is more expensive, so buy less and use more vegetables to make the meat go further. Trim away as much fat as possible from meat and poultry and remove any skin, before cooking where possible, but always before serving.

✦ Before serving, drain foods cooked in fat on paper towels, to absorb any excess fat.

✦ When making soups or casseroles, skim away any fat which rises to the surface during cooking, and any which forms after cooling. Blot soups with paper towels before serving to soak up any fat.

✦ Nonstick pans and equipment not only make life easier when it comes to cleaning, but enable you to cut down on the amount of fat needed. Remember not to use metal utensils in nonstick pans to avoid damaging the coating - use heat-resistant plastic or wooden implements instead.

✦ Ingredients with a high fat content should be kept to a minimum. Some traditional Chinese ingredients, such as peanut oil, coconut, cashews and other nuts, all of which are used

for their rich flavors, have relatively high levels of saturated fat. Use them in small quantities only, unless you are on a very strict diet, when they should be avoided completely. Shrimp are low in fat, but their cholesterol content is fairly high so they are best eaten in moderation.

HEALTHFUL COOKING METHODS

Steaming

A healthful method of cooking as few of the food's nutrients are lost. Steaming also preserves the color and texture of the ingredients. Use an authentic Chinese bamboo steamer, a metal steamer, or even a large metal strainer. Place in a wok or over a large saucepan of boiling water and cover tightly, to allow the food to cook in the steam. Lay a sheet of parchment paper in the steamer to prevent food sticking to the bottom and never overlap items of food as this will hinder cooking: use two steamers and stack one on top of the other.

Stir-Frying

Using a minimal amount of oil, stir-frying is also a healthful way to cook food, and if you use a nonstick wok even smaller quantities of oil are needed. If you prefer to keep with tradition, however, then make sure your steel wok is well seasoned: before you use it for the first time, heat the wok and rub with oil, then always keep it well oiled, cleaning it with water only, not detergent. When cooking meat, heat the oil until very hot, but cook more delicate vegetables and spices over a moderate heat, to avoid burning. Keep the heat constant and keep turning the food with a spatula to ensure the food is evenly cooked and does not absorb too much oil. After the initial searing of the ingredients in the oil, liquid is often added and the food allowed to finish cooking in the steam.

Oven-Cooking

Food is rarely cooked in ovens in Chinese homes, but it is a method often used in restaurants. The most renowned oven-cooking method is 'red-roasting', in which meat, fish or root vegetables are cooked slowly in a combination of spices and dark soy

sauce and with only a little oil. This turns them a deep reddish-brown and gives a delicious rich flavor. Large fish are particularly good when baked in the oven and need few additional ingredients, especially if wrapped in parchment or foil, when they cook largely in their own juices.

Broiling

Foods to be broiled or grilled benefit from being marinated before cooking. This not only adds flavor but will help to keep the foods moist when exposed to direct heat, which is particularly important when using little or no fat.

Braising

Rich, slow-cooked Chinese dishes make a pleasant change to stir-fries. Foods are initially seared in a little oil then further cooked in a liquid such as stock, which is thickened with a paste of cornstarch and water to form a sauce. Cooking in this way ensures nutrients and flavor are retained in the sauce. Always make your own stock for the perfect balance of flavors in your sauces and soups. Ready-made stock, especially in the form of stock cubes, is often very high in salt and artificial flavorings.

SERVING CHINESE DISHES

Attractive presentation is an important part of Chinese cooking. Garnishes and decorations not only make the food look more appetizing, they also enhance the flavor and texture of a dish. Choose garnishes that reflect or complement the ingredients of the dish you are serving: for example a dish containing ground coriander will be enhanced by a garnish of fresh cilantro sprigs, a sprinkling of sesame seeds will complement the flavor of a dish cooked in sesame oil, while chopped chiles will intensify the flavor of a hot, spicy dish. Remember, however, that these finishing touches should not overpower the food and must always be edible.

♦ Green onion flowers are a particularly attractive garnish. Cut the green onion into 2-inch lengths, then make several lengthwise cuts at one or both ends, about 3/4 inch long. Put into a bowl of iced water and leave for 30 minutes. The cut ends will curl outwards to resemble a flower.

♦ To make carrot or daikon flowers, cut evenly spaced grooves along the vegetable with a channel knife or zester, then cut into slices to give flower shapes.

CHINESE INGREDIENTS

Chinese cooking uses many different sauces, pastes, herbs and spices to enhance the flavors of the main ingredients. Such items can all be bought from Chinese food shops and supermarkets and, now that there is an increasing interest in ethnic cooking, many large supermarket chains have their own range of Chinese foods too.

Bamboo Shoots The young shoots of certain varieties of bamboo, they are pale yellow in color with a crunchy texture and fairly bland flavor. Bamboo shoots are available in cans, whole or sliced.

Tofu Low in fat and high in protein, tofu is made from yellow soy beans and has a distinctive soft texture and neutral flavor. It is sold in solid cakes which are kept in water and drained and chopped before use. Handle and cook with care to prevent the tofu breaking up.

Bean Sprouts Widely used in Chinese cooking, these are the sprouting shoots of the mung bean, approximately 2 inches long. They have a mild, watery taste and crisp texture and can be steamed or stir-fried, or eaten raw in small quantities.

Black Beans Small black soy beans, fermented in salt and spices, also available as a paste or a sauce.

Bok Choy Also known as Chinese white cabbage, bok choy has white stems and dark green leaves which grow in small clusters. The stems are succulent and the leaves tender and mildly flavored. It can be served raw or cooked.

Daikon Also known as mooli or Chinese radish, the daikon resembles a large parsnip. The flesh is white, crisp and slightly pungent and can be eaten raw or cooked.

Dried Mushrooms There are several kinds of dried Chinese mushrooms, all of which add a distinctive earthy flavor and aroma to dishes. Soak in hot water for 20 minutes, drain, squeeze dry and discard the tough stem before using.

Noodles There are many varieties available; egg noodles have a higher fat content than rice noodles. Thin, transparent noodles require little cooking and need only be soaked in hot water for a few minutes to separate and soften them before stir-frying.

Rice Vinegar Made from soured and fermented rice wine. White rice vinegar is clear and mild in flavor; red rice vinegar is sweet and spicy.

Rice Wine Made from glutinous rice, yeast and spring water, this wine is used extensively in Chinese cooking. Pale, dry sherry is a good substitute, and if a sweet, spicy flavor is required, sweet sherry can also be used.

Straw Mushrooms Small fleshy mushrooms with domed caps. Available in cans, they should be drained and rinsed before use.

Vegetables Chow-Chow The root of the mustard green, also known as Szechuan preserved vegetables, which is pickled in salt and hot chiles and sold in cans. It has a crunchy texture and adds a spicy flavor to dishes. Rinse before using.

Water Chestnuts Round, white root vegetables about the size of a walnut, they are crunchy in texture with a mild, slightly sweet flavor. They are available fresh from Chinese supermarkets but are more commonly sold in cans. Rinse well before using.

Wonton Skins Thin, pastry-like sheets made from egg and flour. They can be bought fresh or frozen and are available in squares or rounds. They can be kept in the refrigerator, wrapped, for about 5 days.

HERBS AND SPICES

Cinnamon Whole cinnamon sticks are highly aromatic and pungent and should be broken into 2 or 3 pieces before use, to release their flavor. Remove from the dish before serving. Ground cinnamon has a much milder flavor and should only be used as a substitute if very fresh.

Cilantro Fresh cilantro resembles delicate flat-leaf parsley. It is usually sold in large bunches, with the roots left on, but can also be found in supermarkets in small packages or growing in pots. It has a distinctive flavor and smell and is usually added at the end of cooking.

Five-Spice Powder A mixture of ground star anise, Szechuan peppercorns, fennel, cloves and cinnamon, which gives a fragrant, spicy, sweet flavor to dishes.

Fresh Ginger Root Once peeled and chopped or sliced, fresh ginger root adds a sweet, spicy flavor to all kinds of sweet and savoury dishes.

Lemon Grass The long, thin stalks of this herb look similar to green onions. They should be bruised or broken to release their lemony flavor. Grated lemon or lime zest may be substituted.

Star Anise These attractive pods, in the shape of an eight-pointed star, have a mild liquorice flavor. They should be removed from a dish before serving.

Szechuan Peppercorns These mildly spicy, aromatic dried berries should be toasted and crushed or ground before use. To toast, dry-fry in a wok for a few minutes. Crush in a mortar and pestle or grind in a spice grinder.

OILS

Chile Oil Hot, pungent oil that should be heated gently as it burns easily. It is best used as a flavoring rather than a cooking agent.

Peanut Oil A slightly sweet, mild oil that withstands heat very well. Use it in moderation as it has a high saturated fat content.

Sesame Oil A thick, rich oil with a strong nutty flavor. It is best used to add flavor rather than for cooking as it burns easily.

Sunflower Oil This light, mild-flavored oil is high in polyunsaturates and withstands heat well.

SAUCES

Chile Sauce A bright red, hot sauce made from chiles, vinegar, sugar and salt. It can be used in cooking but is more often served as a dip.

Hoisin Sauce This thick, dark reddish-brown sauce is made from soy beans, vinegar, spices, garlic and sugar and gives a sweet flavor to marinades and barbecue sauces.

Oyster Sauce A thick, brown sauce made from concentrated oysters, soy sauce and brine. It is often added to stir-fried dishes, particularly beef.

Plum Sauce This thick, sweet condiment, made from plums, apricots, garlic, vinegar and seasonings is used in cooking or as a dip.

Soy Sauce The essential ingredient in Chinese cooking, soy sauce is made from soy beans, flour and water, which are fermented and aged for several months. Light soy sauce has a full flavor and is rather salty. Dark soy sauce is a darker brown color, thicker and sweeter. When soy sauce is used, additional salt is often not necessary.

Yellow Bean Sauce This thick, spicy, aromatic sauce is made from fermented yellow beans and is quite salty. It is often used in sauces for fish and poultry.

─── CHINESE CHICKEN STOCK ───

1 (2-1/4 to 2-3/4-lb.) chicken, giblets removed
2 slices fresh ginger root
1 garlic clove
2 green onions
Large pinch of salt
Large pinch of ground white pepper

Skin chicken and trim away any visible fat. Wash and place in a large saucepan with remaining ingredients and 9 cups of cold water.

Bring to a boil, skimming away surface scum using a large flat ladle. Reduce heat, cover and simmer 2 hours. Allow to cool slightly.

Line a strainer with clean cheesecloth and place over a large bowl. Ladle stock through strainer and discard chicken and vegetables. Cover and chill. Skim away any fat that forms on surface before using. Store in refrigerator up to 3 days or freeze up to 3 months.

Makes 7-3/4 cups.

Total Cals: 265   Total fat: less than 5 g
Cals per 1/4 cup: 7
Fat per 1/4 cup: trace

CHINESE BEEF STOCK

2 lbs. lean beef chuck
1-inch piece fresh ginger root, peeled
1 garlic clove
2 shallots
1 stalk celery
2 carrots
2 tablespoons dark soy sauce
Large pinch of salt
Large pinch of freshly ground pepper

Trim any visible fat and silver skin from beef. Cut into 2-inch pieces. Wash and pat dry with paper towels.

Place beef in a large saucepan with remaining ingredients and 9 cups of cold water. Bring to a boil, skimming away surface scum using a large, flat ladle. Reduce heat, cover and simmer 2 hours. Allow to cool slightly.

Line a strainer with clean cheesecloth and place over a large bowl. Ladle stock through strainer and discard beef and vegetables. Cover and chill. Skim away any fat that forms on surface before using. Store in refrigerator up to 3 days or freeze up to 3 months.

Makes 8-1/4 cups.

Total Cals: 464   Total fat: less than 5 g
Cals per 1/4 cup: 9
Fat per 1/4 cup: less than 1 g

—CHINESE VEGETABLE STOCK—

1 stalk lemon grass
2 slices fresh ginger root
1 garlic clove
2 green onions
1 large carrot, sliced
2 stalks celery
4 oz. bean sprouts
Large pinch of salt
Large pinch of ground white pepper

Break lemon grass to release its flavor and place in a large saucepan with 9 cups of cold water and all remaining ingredients.

Bring to a boil, skimming away surface scum using a large, flat ladle. Reduce heat, cover and simmer 45 minutes. Allow to cool slightly.

Line a strainer with clean cheesecloth and place over a large bowl. Ladle stock through strainer and discard vegetables. Cover and store in refrigerator up to 3 days or freeze up to 3 months.

Makes 7 cups.

Total Cals: 188   Total fat: trace
Cals per 1/4 cup: 4
Fat per 1/4 cup: trace

– CHICKEN & ASPARAGUS SOUP –

8 oz. fresh asparagus
4-1/2 cups Chinese Chicken Stock, page 12
2 tablespoons light soy sauce
2 tablespoons dry sherry
2 teaspoons brown sugar
2 oz. vermicelli rice noodles
1/2-inch piece fresh ginger root, peeled and chopped
12 oz. lean cooked chicken, finely shredded
Salt and ground white pepper
2 green onions, finely chopped, to garnish

Trim ends from asparagus spears and slice spears into 1-1/2-inch pieces. Pour stock into a large saucepan along with soy sauce and sherry. Stir in brown sugar. Bring to a boil and add asparagus and noodles. Simmer, covered, 5 or 6 minutes.

Stir in chopped ginger and shredded chicken and season with salt and pepper. Simmer 3 or 4 minutes to heat through. Garnish with chopped green onions and serve.

Makes 4 servings.

Total Cals: 972   Total fat: 17.3 g
Cals per portion: 243   Fat per portion: 4.25 g

—CHICKEN DUMPLING SOUP—

8 oz. lean ground chicken
1 tablespoon light soy sauce
3 tablespoons chopped fresh chives
1 garlic clove, finely chopped
2 egg whites
1 teaspoon sugar
Salt and freshly ground pepper
16 wonton skins
4-1/2 cups Chinese Chicken Stock, page 12
2 tablespoons rice wine

In a bowl, mix chicken, soy sauce, 1 tablespoon of the chives and the garlic. Bind together with 1 egg white and stir in sugar, salt and pepper.

Place a little of the chicken mixture in center of each wonton skin, brush edges with egg white and bring corners together, pinching edges to seal. Cook dumplings in a large pan of boiling water 1 minute. Drain. Bring stock to a boil and stir in rice wine, dumplings and remaining chives. Simmer 2 minutes. Serve immediately.

Makes 4 servings.

Total Cals: 842
Cals per portion: 210

Total fat: 14.9 g
Fat per portion: 3.7 g

—HOT & SOUR TURKEY SOUP—

4 oz. lean ground turkey
1 oz. dried Chinese mushrooms, soaked in hot water
   20 minutes
4 oz. vegetable chow-chow, shredded
4-1/2 cups Chinese Chicken Stock, page 12
2 teaspoons brown sugar
2 tablespoons red rice vinegar
Large pinch of ground white pepper
1 tablespoon dark soy sauce
2 teaspoons cornstarch blended with 4 teaspoons
   water
2 green onions, finely chopped
2 tablespoons chopped fresh cilantro

Cook turkey in a saucepan of boiling water 3 minutes. Drain and set aside. Drain mushrooms and squeeze out excess water. Discard stems and slice caps.

Place all ingredients, except cornstarch mixture, green onions and cilantro, in a saucepan. Bring to a boil and simmer 3 minutes. Add the cornstarch mixture and cook, stirring, until thickened. Add chopped green onions and cilantro and serve.

Makes 4 servings.

Total Cals: 423   Total fat: 7.8 g
Cals per portion: 106   Fat per portion: 1.9 g

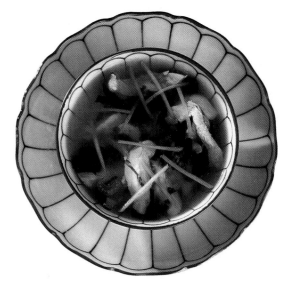

—CHICKEN & BOK CHOY SOUP—

6 oz. lean chicken
6 oz. bok choy
4-1/2 cups Chinese Chicken Stock, page 12
1-inch piece fresh ginger root, peeled and finely
    chopped
2 tablespoons rice wine
1 tablespoon light soy sauce
Salt and freshly ground pepper
Strips of fresh ginger root, to garnish

Cut chicken into thin strips. Cook in a saucepan of boiling water 2 minutes until just firm and opaque. Drain.

Trim and shred bok choy. Cook in a saucepan of boiling water 20 seconds or until wilted. Rinse in cold water and drain.

Pour stock into a saucepan and stir in chopped ginger, wine and soy sauce. Bring to a boil, reduce to a simmer and add prepared bok choy and chicken. Simmer 5 minutes, season with salt and pepper and serve garnished with ginger strips.

Makes 4 servings.

Total Cals: 420   Total fat: 5.1 g
Cals per portion: 105   Fat per portion: 1.3 g

BLACK-EYED PEA SOUP

6 oz. black-eyed peas
1 large carrot
4 oz. daikon, peeled
1 bunch green onions
4-1/2 cups Chinese Vegetable Stock, page 14
2 tablespoons light soy sauce
2 garlic cloves, finely chopped
1 fresh red chile, seeded and finely chopped
Salt and freshly ground pepper
Carrot and daikon flowers, to garnish

Place peas in a saucepan, add enough water to cover and bring to a boil. Cover and simmer 45 minutes or until tender. Drain and rinse. Cut carrots and daikon into thin strips. Cut green onions into fine shreds.

Pour stock into a saucepan and stir in soy sauce. Bring to a boil and add prepared vegetables, garlic and chile. Simmer 4 minutes, then add peas. Season with salt and pepper and cook 3 minutes. Skim surface, garnish and serve.

Makes 4 servings.

Total Cals: 711   Total fat: 3.3 g
Cals per portion: 178   Fat per portion: 0.8 g

— THREE MUSHROOM SOUP —

4 dried Chinese mushrooms, soaked in hot water
  20 minutes
1 oz. oyster mushrooms
2 oz. button mushrooms
4-1/2 cups Chinese Vegetable Stock, page 14
1/2-inch piece fresh ginger root, peeled and finely
  chopped
1 garlic clove, finely chopped
2 tablespoons dry sherry
2 tablespoons dark soy sauce
4 oz. fresh tofu, drained and diced
2 teaspoons cornstarch mixed with 4 teaspoons water
2 tablespoons shredded basil leaves

Drain soaked mushrooms and squeeze out excess water. Discard stems and slice caps. Slice oyster mushrooms and cut button mushrooms in half.

Pour stock into a saucepan and add ginger, garlic, sherry and soy sauce. Bring to a boil, reduce heat and carefully stir in mushrooms and tofu. Simmer 5 minutes then add cornstarch mixture and cook, stirring, another 2 minutes or until thickened. Stir in basil and serve.

Makes 4 servings.

Total Cals: 304	Total fat: 4.6 g
Cals per portion: 76	Fat per portion: 1.1 g

—— CRAB & CORN SOUP ——

8 oz. baby corn
1/2-inch piece fresh ginger root, peeled and finely
   chopped
1 garlic clove, finely chopped
6 oz. crab meat, picked over
2 tablespoons rice wine
1 tablespoon light soy sauce
4-1/2 cups Chinese Vegetable Stock, page 14
Salt and ground white pepper
2 teaspoons cornstarch mixed with 4 teaspoons
   water
2 green onions, shredded, to garnish

Bring a small saucepan of water to a boil, add baby corn and cook 3 or 4 minutes or until just softened. Drain. In a bowl, mix together ginger, garlic, crab meat, rice wine and soy sauce.

Pour stock into a saucepan, bring to a boil and add corn and crab mixture. Simmer 5 minutes. Season with salt and pepper, add cornstarch mixture and cook, stirring, until thickened. Garnish with green onions and serve.

Makes 4 servings.

Total Cals: 347   Total fat: 2.1 g
Cals per portion: 87   Fat per portion: 0.5 g

—SPINACH & MONKFISH SOUP—

6 oz. fresh spinach
1 lb. monkfish, skinned
4-1/2 cups Chinese Vegetable Stock, page 14
1 tablespoon light soy sauce
1 teaspoon chile sauce
1 teaspoon brown sugar
Salt and freshly ground pepper
2 tablespoons chopped fresh cilantro
Cilantro leaves, to garnish

Remove spinach stems and wash leaves. Cook leaves in a saucepan of boiling water 20 seconds or until just wilted. Drain and rinse in cold water.

Cut monkfish into 3/4-inch chunks. Cook in a saucepan of boiling water 2 minutes or until firm and opaque. Drain.

Pour stock into a saucepan. Stir in the soy sauce, chile sauce, sugar, salt and pepper. Bring to a boil, add spinach and monkfish and simmer 5 minutes. Stir in chopped cilantro and cook another 2 minutes. Garnish with cilantro and serve.

Makes 4 servings.

Total Cals: 521   Total fat: 10.3 g
Cals per portion: 130   Fat per portion: 2.6 g

-BEEF & WATER CHESTNUT SOUP-

12 oz. lean beef round or sirloin steak
4-1/2 cups Chinese Beef Stock, page 13
1 whole cinnamon stick, broken
2 star anise
2 tablespoons dark soy sauce
2 tablespoons dry sherry
3 tablespoons tomato paste
1 or 2 tablespoons chile sauce
1 (4-oz.) can water chestnuts, rinsed and sliced
2 green onions, chopped, to garnish

Trim away any fat from beef and cut into thin strips.

Place all ingredients except green onions in a large saucepan. Bring to a boil, skimming away surface scum with a flat ladle. Cover and simmer 20 minutes or until beef is tender.

Skim soup again and discard cinnamon stick and star anise. Blot surface with paper towels to remove fat. Garnish with green onions and serve.

Makes 4 servings.

Total Cals: 691	Total fat: 15.8 g
Cals per portion: 173	Fat per portion: 3.9 g

—— BEEF & EGG DROP SOUP ——

1 tablespoon dark soy sauce
8 oz. extra-lean ground beef
1 garlic clove, crushed
1 whole cinnamon stick, broken
2 tablespoons tomato paste
Ground white pepper
4-1/2 cups Chinese Beef Stock, page 13
2 teaspoons cornstarch mixed with 4 teaspoons
   water
1 egg white, lightly beaten
2 tablespoons chopped fresh cilantro, to garnish

In a nonstick or well-seasoned wok, heat soy
sauce, add beef, garlic and cinnamon stick
and stir-fry 3 or 4 minutes or until beef is
browned all over. Drain well on paper
towels. Transfer beef mixture to a large
saucepan and stir in the tomato paste and
white pepper. Pour in stock and bring to a
boil, skimming away surface scum with a flat
ladle. Cover and simmer 20 minutes.

Discard cinnamon stick. Add cornstarch
mixture and cook, stirring, until thickened.
With soup still simmering, pour in the egg
white in a thin stream, stirring until thin
strands of egg form in the soup. Garnish with
cilantro and serve.

Makes 4 servings.

Total Cals: 545   Total fat: 11.2 g
Cals per portion: 136   Fat per portion: 2.8 g

BEEF & RICE SOUP

8 oz. lean beef round or sirloin steak
1 tablespoon dark soy sauce
1 garlic clove, finely chopped
2 star anise
1/4 cup dry sherry
1/4 cup long-grain white rice, rinsed
4-1/2 cups Chinese Beef Stock, page 13
2 tablespoons hoisin sauce
2 tablespoons oyster sauce
2 green onions, shredded, to garnish

Trim any fat from beef and cut beef into thin strips.

In a nonstick or well-seasoned wok, heat the soy sauce and stir-fry beef, garlic and star anise 3 or 4 minutes. Transfer to a saucepan and add remaining ingredients except the green onions. Bring to a boil, skimming away scum with a flat ladle. Cover and simmer 25 minutes. Discard star anise. Garnish with green onions and serve.

Makes 4 servings.

Total Cals: 793   Total fat: 12.2 g
Cals per portion: 198   Fat per portion: 3.05 g

— SHRIMP WITH GINGER DIP —

16 uncooked large shrimp, peeled, with tails left on
Cilantro leaves and fresh ginger root strips, to
   garnish
MARINADE:
1 tablespoon light soy sauce
1 teaspoon rice wine
1 teaspoon sesame oil
1 garlic clove, crushed
DIP:
1 tablespoon white rice vinegar
1 teaspoon sugar
2 tablespoons chopped fresh cilantro
1/2-inch piece fresh ginger root, peeled and finely
   chopped

Using a small sharp knife, cut along the back
of each shrimp and remove the thin black
cord. Rinse and dry shrimp with paper
towels and place on a plate. Mix together
marinade ingredients and brush over shrimp.
Cover and chill 1 hour.

Mix together ingredients for dip, cover and
chill. Preheat broiler. Place shrimp on a
broiler rack and cook 1 or 2 minutes on each
side, basting with marinade, until cooked
through. Garnish with cilantro leaves and
ginger strips and serve with the dip.

Makes 4 servings.

Total Cals: 276   Total fat: 8.1 g
Cals per portion: 69   Fat per portion: 2.02 g

CHILE SHRIMP BALLS

1 lb. cooked, peeled large shrimp, thawed and dried,
  if frozen
1 fresh red chile, seeded and chopped
3 green onions, finely chopped
Grated zest of 1 small lemon
2 tablespoons cornstarch
1 egg white, lightly beaten
Salt and freshly ground pepper
Strips of fresh red chile, to garnish

Place all the ingredients except the garnish in
a blender or food processor and process to
form a firm dough-like mixture.

Divide the shrimp mixture into 12 portions
and form each portion into a smooth ball,
flouring the hands with extra cornstarch if
necessary, to prevent sticking.

Bring a wok or large saucepan of water to a
boil, arrange shrimp balls on a layer of
parchment paper in a steamer and place over
water. Cover and steam 5 minutes or until
cooked through. Garnish with sliced chile
and serve on a bed of shredded napa cabbage
and watercress.

Makes 4 servings.

Total Cals: 574   Total fat: 8.2 g
Cals per portion: 144   Fat per portion: 2.05 g

—STEAMED FISH DUMPLINGS—

6 oz. skinless cod fillet
1 slice lean bacon, trimmed of fat and finely
**   chopped**
1 teaspoon light soy sauce
1 teaspoon oyster sauce
1 tablespoon chopped fresh chives
1 teaspoon cornstarch
12 round wonton skins
1 egg white, lightly beaten
Chopped fresh chives, to garnish

Place all the ingredients except the wonton skins, egg white and garnish in a blender or food processor and process to form a firm mixture. Divide into 12 portions.

Place a portion of filling in the center of each wonton skin and lightly brush the edges of the wonton skin with egg white.

Fold over to form crescent shapes and crimp edges to seal. Bring a wok or large saucepan of water to a boil, arrange dumplings on a layer of parchment paper in a steamer and place over water. Cover and steam 10 minutes or until cooked through. Garnish with chives and serve on a bed of sliced lotus root and red bell pepper.

Makes 4 servings.

Total Cals: 482   Total fat: 8.9 g
Cals per portion: 121   Fat per portion: 2.22 g

—PEARL PATTIES & SHERRY DIP—

3/4 cup long-grain white rice
12 oz. extra-lean ground beef
2 green onions, finely chopped
1 garlic clove, crushed
1 tablespoon dark soy sauce
1 tablespoon dry sherry
2 teaspoons cornstarch
DIP:
2 tablespoons dry sherry
2 tablespoons dark soy sauce
1 teaspoon sugar
1 garlic clove, crushed

Place rice in a bowl, add enough water to cover and soak 1 hour. Drain well and dry on a clean cloth. Mix together beef, green onions, garlic, soy sauce, sherry and cornstarch to form a firm mixture. Divide into 16 portions and shape into 1-1/2-inch diameter patties.

Press each patty into the rice to coat on both sides. Bring a wok or large saucepan of water to a boil. Arrange patties on a layer of parchment paper in a steamer, making sure they don't overlap - you will probably need 2 steamers. Place over water, cover and steam 20 minutes. Mix together ingredients for dip and serve with the patties.

Makes 4 servings.

Total Cals: 1138   Total fat: 17.4 g
Cals per portion: 284   Fat per portion: 4.35 g

——SESAME SHRIMP SALAD——

8 oz. snow peas
2 oz. oyster mushrooms, thinly sliced
1 (4-oz.) can water chestnuts, rinsed and sliced
8 oz. cooked, peeled large shrimp, thawed and
    dried, if frozen
2 tablespoons sesame seeds
DRESSING:
1 tablespoon sesame oil
1 tablespoon light soy sauce
2 teaspoons white rice vinegar
1 teaspoon brown sugar
Salt and freshly ground pepper

Remove ends from snow peas and string if necessary. Bring a saucepan of water to a boil and cook 2 minutes or until just softened. Drain and rinse under cold water. Drain and leave to cool completely.

Mix together the sliced mushrooms, water chestnuts, shrimp and sesame seeds. Stir in the cooled snow peas. Mix together the dressing ingredients and pour over the salad just before serving.

Makes 4 servings.

Total Cals: 642   Total fat: 23.2 g
Cals per portion: 160   Fat per portion: 5.8 g

—STUFFED WHITE LACE CREPES—

3 egg whites, lightly beaten
1/4 cup cornstarch
3 tablespoons Chinese Vegetable Stock, page 14
1 teaspoon peanut oil
Lemon twists and strips of fresh ginger root, to
    garnish
FILLING:
6 oz. small broccoli flowerets, blanched
8 oz. cooked, shelled mussels
1/2-inch piece fresh ginger root, peeled and finely
    chopped
2 tablespoons light soy sauce
1 tablespoon rice wine
4 teaspoons black bean sauce

In a small bowl, mix together the egg whites,
cornstarch and stock. Brush a small nonstick
or well-seasoned crepe pan with oil and heat
until hot. Drizzle surface with one-quarter of
the mixture to give a lacey effect. Cook a few
seconds or until set. Carefully lift out, drain
on paper towels and keep warm. Repeat with
remaining batter, to make 4 crepes.

Place all filling ingredients in a saucepan
and mix gently. Cook over low heat 3 or 4
minutes until warmed through. Arrange one-
quarter of the filling on cooked side of each
crepe and roll up. Garnish with lemon twists
and ginger strips and serve.

Makes 4 servings.

Total Cals: 508   Total fat: 6.1 g
Cals per portion: 127   Fat per portion: 1.52 g

— BROILED FIVE-SPICE CHICKEN —

2 boneless, skinless chicken breasts, each weighing
   6 oz., trimmed
2 small red bell peppers, halved
2 small yellow bell peppers, halved
Chopped fresh chives, to garnish
MARINADE:
1 garlic clove, crushed
1 fresh red chile, seeded and chopped
3 tablespoons light soy sauce
1 teaspoon five-spice powder
1 teaspoon brown sugar
2 teaspoons sesame oil

Using a small sharp knife, score chicken
breasts on both sides in a crisscross pattern,
taking care not to slice all way through. Place
in a shallow dish with the bell peppers. Mix
together the marinade ingredients, pour over
the chicken and bell peppers and turn to
coat. Cover and chill 1 hour.

Preheat broiler. Remove chicken and bell
peppers from marinade, place on broiler rack
and broil 4 or 5 minutes on each side, basting
with marinade, or until chicken is cooked
through. Slice chicken breasts and serve with
a piece of red and yellow bell pepper,
garnished with chives.

Makes 4 servings.

Total Cals: 590   Total fat: 14.5 g
Cals per portion: 148   Fat per portion: 3.62 g

—MARINATED MUSHROOMS—

1 oz. dried Chinese mushrooms, soaked in hot water
   20 minutes
4 oz. oyster mushrooms
4 oz. button mushrooms
1 tablespoon sunflower oil
2 tablespoons light soy sauce
2 stalks celery, chopped
2 garlic cloves, thinly sliced
1 whole cinnamon stick, broken
Chopped celery leaves, to garnish
MARINADE:
3 tablespoons light soy sauce
3 tablespoons dry sherry
Freshly ground pepper

Drain Chinese mushrooms and squeeze out excess water. Discard stems and thinly slice caps. Slice oyster and button mushrooms. Heat oil in a nonstick or well-seasoned wok and stir-fry all the mushrooms 2 minutes.

Add remaining ingredients except marinade and garnish and stir-fry 2 or 3 minutes or until just cooked. Transfer to a shallow dish and let cool. Mix together marinade ingredients and pour over cooled mushroom mixture. Cover and chill 1 hour. Discard cinnamon stick, garnish and serve on a bed of bean sprouts and shredded napa cabbage.

Makes 4 servings.

Total Cals: 366   Total fat: 16.3 g
Cals per portion: 92   Fat per portion: 4.07 g

—— CHILE CUCUMBER SALAD ——

1 (1-lb.) cucumber
2 teaspoons salt
1 green bell pepper
2 tablespoons sesame seeds
Strips of fresh red chile, to garnish
DRESSING:
2 shallots, finely chopped
1 fresh red chile, seeded and chopped
3 tablespoons white rice vinegar
1 tablespoon rice wine
2 teaspoons sugar
2 teaspoons light soy sauce
1 teaspoon sesame oil

Peel cucumber and slice very thinly. Place in a bowl, sprinkle with salt and set aside 15 minutes. Remove seeds from bell pepper, halve and thinly slice lengthwise.

Mix together dressing ingredients. Rinse the cucumber slices, drain well and pat dry with paper towels. Place in a bowl and carefully mix in green bell pepper. Add dressing, cover and chill 1 hour. Mix well, sprinkle with sesame seeds, garnish with chile strips and serve.

Makes 4 servings.

Total Cals: 294   Total fat: 15.2 g
Cals per portion: 74   Fat per portion: 3.8 g

GINGERED MELONS

1/2 honeydew melon
1/2 cantaloupe melon
1 (4-oz.) can water chestnuts, rinsed
1-inch piece fresh ginger root, peeled and finely
**   chopped**
1/4 cup dry sherry
4 pieces stem ginger in syrup, sliced
2 tablespoons dried melon seeds

Using a spoon, scoop out the seeds from both melons. Cut in half, peel away skin and thinly slice melon flesh. Slice water chestnuts.

Arrange melon slices on serving plates and top with sliced water chestnuts.

Mix together chopped ginger, dry sherry and stem ginger with its syrup and spoon over melon and water chestnuts. Cover and chill 30 minutes. Sprinkle with melon seeds and serve.

Makes 4 servings.

Total Cals: 428   Total fat: 10.9 g
Cals per portion: 107   Fat per portion: 2.72 g

─────STUFFED RED MULLET─────

2 oz. oyster mushrooms
2 oz. cooked, peeled large shrimp, thawed and
  dried, if frozen
Grated zest of 1 small lemon
2 tablespoons oyster sauce
4 red mullet or red snapper, each weighing about 8
  oz., cleaned and scaled
1/4 cup dry sherry
1 large carrot, cut into thin strips
1 daikon, peeled and cut into thin strips
8 oz. small broccoli flowerets
Lemon zest and chopped green onions, to garnish

Finely chop mushrooms and shrimp. Place in a small bowl and mix in lemon zest. Stir in oyster sauce and set aside. Rinse fish and pat dry with paper towels. Divide mushroom mixture into 4 portions and press into cavity of each fish. Place stuffed fish in a shallow dish and spoon sherry over fish. Cover and chill 30 minutes.

Bring a wok or large saucepan of water to a boil. Arrange the vegetables on parchment paper in 2 steamers, lay fish on top and spoon over sherry marinade. Place over water, cover and steam 10 minutes. Carefully turn fish over and steam another 8 to 10 minutes or until cooked through. Garnish and serve.

Makes 4 servings.

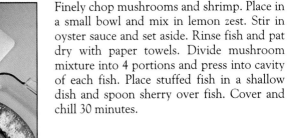

Total Cals: 1024   Total fat: 18.3 g
Cals per portion: 256   Fat per portion: 4.6 g

STEAMED FISH CAKES

1/2-inch piece fresh ginger root, peeled and chopped
1-1/2 lbs. cod fillets, skinned and chopped
1 egg white, lightly beaten
2 teaspoons cornstarch
2 tablespoons chopped fresh chives
Salt and ground white pepper
4 oz. oyster mushrooms
2 shallots
2 zucchini
1 red bell pepper, halved
1 yellow bell pepper, halved
1/2-inch piece fresh ginger root, peeled
1 garlic clove
Fresh chives, to garnish

Put chopped ginger, cod, egg white,
cornstarch, chopped chives, salt and pepper
in a food processor or blender and process
until finely chopped. Divide into 12 portions
and shape into 3-inch diameter patties. Line a
large plate with parchment paper, arrange
fish cakes on plate, cover and chill 30
minutes. Using a sharp knife, thinly slice
mushrooms, shallots, zucchini, bell peppers,
remaining ginger and garlic.

Bring a wok or large saucepan of water to a
boil. Arrange vegetables on parchment paper
in a steamer, place fish cakes on top and
place over water. Cover and steam 10
minutes or until cooked, turning fish cakes
halfway through. Garnish with chives and
serve with a salad and oyster sauce.

Makes 4 servings.

Total Cals: 647   Total fat: 6.2 g
Cals per portion: 162   Fat per portion: 1.55 g

—SPICY RICE WITH MONKFISH—

2 teaspoons sunflower oil
1 teaspoon chile oil
1 garlic clove, finely chopped
1 whole cinnamon stick, broken
2 star anise
1-1/4 cups long-grain white rice, rinsed
3-1/2 cups Chinese Vegetable Stock, page 14
Salt and freshly ground pepper
1 lb. monkfish tails, skinned and cut into chunks
8 oz. cooked, shelled mussels
6 green onions, chopped
Grated zest of 1 lime
Strips of lime zest, to garnish

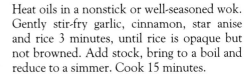

Heat oils in a nonstick or well-seasoned wok. Gently stir-fry garlic, cinnamon, star anise and rice 3 minutes, until rice is opaque but not browned. Add stock, bring to a boil and reduce to a simmer. Cook 15 minutes.

Season with salt and pepper and stir in monkfish. Simmer 10 minutes or until most of the liquid has been absorbed. Gently stir in remaining ingredients except garnish and heat through 3 or 4 minutes. Discard cinnamon and star anise, garnish with strips of lime zest and serve with a mixed salad.

Makes 4 servings.

Total Cals: 1816   Total fat: 31.4 g
Cals per portion: 454   Fat per portion: 7.85 g

—BAKED TROUT WITH GINGER—

2 trout, each weighing 10 oz., cleaned
Salt and freshly ground pepper
2 green onions, finely shredded
1 tablespoon chopped fresh cilantro
Strips of fresh red chile, to garnish
SAUCE:
1 garlic clove, finely chopped
1/2-inch piece fresh ginger root, peeled and finely
    chopped
2 tablespoons white rice vinegar
2 tablespoons light soy sauce
2 tablespoons dry sherry
1 teaspoon salt
1 teaspoon chile powder
2 teaspoons sugar

Preheat oven to 350F (175C). Rinse trout and pat dry with paper towels. Season trout inside and out with salt and pepper. Fill the cavities with green onions and cilantro. Using a sharp knife, score flesh lightly in diagonal lines. Place trout in a nonstick roasting pan.

Mix together sauce ingredients and pour over trout. Cover loosely with oiled foil and bake 20 minutes, basting halfway through. Remove foil, baste, and bake, uncovered, 10 minutes. Skin trout and remove flesh from bones to give 4 fillets. Brush with cooking juices, garnish with strips of chile and serve with noodles and vegetables.

Makes 4 servings.

Total Cals: 628   Total fat: 17.1 g
Cals per portion: 157   Fat per portion: 4.3 g

—SALMON WITH GINGER DIP—

4 salmon fillets, each weighing 6 oz., skinned
2 tablespoons light soy sauce
1 tablespoon dry sherry
1-inch piece fresh ginger root, peeled and cut into
    thin strips
1 teaspoon sunflower oil
Freshly ground pepper
4 green onions, shredded, to garnish
DIP:
2 tablespoons sweet sherry
1 tablespoon light soy sauce

Using a sharp knife, lightly score the top of
the salmon fillets in diagonal lines, taking
care not to slice all way through.

Place salmon in a shallow dish. Mix together
soy sauce, sherry and ginger strips and spoon
over salmon. Cover and chill 1 hour.

Preheat broiler. Brush broiler rack lightly
with oil. Remove salmon from marinade and
place on rack. Season with pepper and broil
2 or 3 minutes on each side. Meanwhile, mix
together ingredients for dip and set aside.
Drain salmon on paper towels. Garnish with
green onions and serve with dip and
asparagus tips.

Makes 4 servings.

Total Cals: 1163   Total fat: 68.6 g
Cals per portion: 291   Fat per portion: 17.1 g

—FIVE-SPICE SALMON STEAKS—

4 salmon steaks, each weighing 6 oz.
2 teaspoons five-spice powder
Freshly ground pepper
1 tablespoon peanut oil
1 garlic clove, finely chopped
2 tablespoons rice wine
1 tablespoon light soy sauce
1 teaspoon sesame oil
Zest of 1 lemon, cut into fine strips

Rinse salmon steaks and pat dry with paper towels. Rub both sides with five-spice powder and freshly ground pepper.

Heat oil in a nonstick or well-seasoned wok, add garlic and salmon and cook 1 or 2 minutes on each side until salmon is lightly browned.

Add the rice wine, soy sauce and sesame oil and simmer 3 or 4 minutes or until salmon is just cooked through. Stir in lemon zest. Remove salmon with a slotted spoon and remove skin. Serve with wedges of lemon and steamed vegetables.

Makes 4 servings.

Total Cals: 1104   Total fat: 74.2 g
Cals per portion: 276   Fat per portion: 18.5 g

— COD WITH OYSTER SAUCE —

1 (1-1/2-lb.) piece cod fillet, skinned
2 shallots, shredded
4 oz. oyster mushrooms, shredded
2 garlic cloves, finely sliced
4 oz. cooked, peeled large shrimp, thawed and
    dried, if frozen
1/4 cup oyster sauce
2 tablespoons dry sherry
Salt and freshly ground pepper
Grated zest of 1 lime and 1 lemon
2 tablespoons chopped fresh cilantro

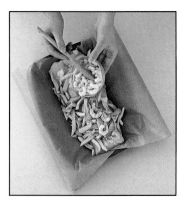

Preheat oven to 350F (175C). Rinse cod fillet
and pat dry with paper towels. Place on a
large piece of parchment paper and put in a
roasting pan. Top cod with shallots,
mushrooms, garlic and shrimp then drizzle
with oyster sauce and sherry. Season with
salt and freshly ground pepper.

Bring ends of the parchment paper over the
fish and pleat together to seal. Bake 25
minutes or until cod is cooked through.
Carefully lift from paper, sprinkle with lime
and lemon zest and cilantro and serve with
rice and salad.

Makes 4 servings.

Total Cals: 717   Total fat: 6.8 g
Cals per portion: 179   Fat per portion: 1.7 g

— COD WITH VINEGAR SAUCE —

1 tablespoon sunflower oil
6 shallots, sliced
2 tablespoons white rice vinegar
2 teaspoons sugar
1 tablespoon light soy sauce
1-1/4 cups Chinese Vegetable Stock, page 14
1 teaspoon cornstarch mixed with 2 teaspoons water
4 cod steaks, each weighing 6 oz.
Salt and freshly ground pepper
2 tablespoons chopped fresh chives

Heat half oil in a nonstick or well-seasoned wok and stir-fry shallots 2 or 3 minutes.

Add vinegar, sugar and soy sauce and stir-fry 1 minute. Pour in stock and bring to a boil. Simmer 8 or 9 minutes or until thickened and slightly reduced. Stir in cornstarch mixture and cook, stirring, until thickened. Keep warm.

Preheat broiler or grill. Season cod steaks on both sides and place on broiler rack. Brush with remaining oil and cook 4 minutes on each side or until cooked through. Drain on paper towels. Remove skin. Stir chives into vinegar sauce, spoon over cod steaks and serve with noodles and broiled tomatoes.

Makes 4 servings.

Total Cals: 616
Cals per portion: 154

Total fat: 18.1 g
Fat per portion: 4.5 g

——SMOKY GARLIC FISH STEW——

1-1/2 lbs. firm white fish fillets, such as cod or
   monkfish, skinned and cut into 1-inch cubes
2 teaspoons light soy sauce
3 tablespoons sweet sherry
1 tablespoon cornstarch
4 large garlic cloves
1 tablespoon sunflower oil
8 oz. shallots, sliced
2 tablespoons fermented black beans
4 green onions, cut into 1-inch pieces
2 tablespoons dark soy sauce

In a bowl, mix together the cubed fish, light
soy sauce, sherry and cornstarch. Roughly
chop the garlic and add to the fish mixture.
Cover and chill 30 minutes. Heat oil in a
nonstick or well-seasoned wok and stir-fry
fish mixture and shallots 3 minutes or until
fish is lightly colored. Remove with a slotted
spoon, drain on paper towels and set aside.

Add remaining ingredients to wok and stir-
fry 2 or 3 minutes over high heat or until
thick and syrupy. Replace fish mixture and
cook 2 minutes, stirring gently. Serve
immediately with noodles and salad.

Makes 4 servings.

Total Cals: 938   Total fat: 20.1 g
Cals per portion: 234   Fat per portion: 5 g

— LIME BROILED FISH KEBABS —

**12 oz. monkfish tails, skinned and cut into 3/4-inch
    cubes
12 oz. trout fillets, skinned and cut into 3/4-inch
    pieces
2 limes
1 teaspoon sesame oil
Large pinch of five-spice powder
Freshly ground pepper
Strips of lime zest, to garnish**

Place monkfish and trout in a shallow dish.
Juice one of the limes and grate the zest. Mix
juice and zest with sesame oil and five-spice
powder, pour over fish, cover and chill 30
minutes.

Soak 4 bamboo skewers in cold water. Halve
and quarter remaining lime lengthwise, and
then halve each quarter to make 8 wedges.
Slice each piece of lime in half crosswise to
make 16 small pieces.

Preheat broiler. Thread monkfish, trout and
lime pieces onto skewers and place on broiler
rack. Brush with marinade and season with
pepper. Broil 2 minutes on each side,
brushing occasionally with marinade to
prevent drying out. Drain on paper towels,
garnish with lime zest and serve with rice,
vegetables and lime wedges.

Makes 4 servings.

Total Cals: 662	Total fat: 20.8 g
Cals per portion: 156	Fat per portion: 5.2 g

CURRIED CRAB

1-1/2 lbs. cooked large crab claws, thawed and
   dried, if frozen
1 tablespoon sunflower oil
2 garlic cloves, thinly sliced
1 large green bell pepper, shredded
8 oz. small broccoli flowerets
5 tablespoons Chinese Vegetable Stock, page 14
1 tablespoon Madras curry paste
1 tablespoon light soy sauce
1 teaspoon brown sugar

Wrap the end of a rolling pin in plastic
wrap and tap the main part of the crab claws
until the shell cracks, leaving pincers intact.
Peel away hard shell to expose crab flesh,
leaving shell on pincers. Heat oil in a
nonstick or well-seasoned wok and stir-fry
crab and garlic 1 or 2 minutes or until crab is
lightly browned. Drain on paper towels and
set aside.

Mix together remaining ingredients and add
to wok. Simmer 5 minutes, stirring
occasionally. Return crab and garlic to wok
and simmer 2 or 3 minutes, stirring to coat
crab with sauce. Serve immediately with rice,
vegetables and lemon wedges.

Makes 4 servings.

Total Cals: 518   Total fat: 27.2 g
Cals per portion: 129   Fat per portion: 6.8 g

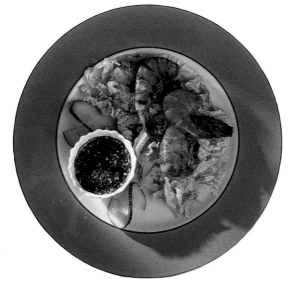

SALT & PEPPER SHRIMP

16 uncooked large shrimp
1 teaspoon chile powder
1 teaspoon coarse sea salt
1 teaspoon Szechuan peppercorns, crushed
2 garlic cloves, finely chopped
1 tablespoon peanut oil
DIP:
1/2 teaspoon Szechuan peppercorns, toasted
  and ground
2 tablespoons light soy sauce
2 tablespoons dry sherry
1 teaspoon brown sugar

Cut off the heads of the shrimp. Use scissors to remove legs, leaving shells.

Rinse shrimp and pat dry with paper towels. In a bowl, mix together shrimp, chile powder, salt, peppercorns and garlic. Heat oil in a nonstick or well-seasoned wok until very hot and stir-fry shrimp 2 or 3 minutes or until shrimp are pink and cooked through. Drain on paper towels.

Mix together ingredients for dip. Serve the shrimp immediately with the dip and a salad.

Makes 4 servings.

Total Cals: 623   Total fat: 19 g
Cals per portion: 156   Fat per portion: 4.75 g

Note: Serve with a finger bowl of water and lemon slices, to freshen the hands.

STIR-FRIED SCALLOPS

1 lb. fresh bay scallops, cleaned and trimmed
8 oz. baby corn
8 oz. snow peas
1 tablespoon sunflower oil
2 shallots, chopped
1 garlic clove, finely chopped
1/2-inch piece fresh ginger root, peeled and finely
    chopped
2 tablespoons yellow bean sauce
1 tablespoon light soy sauce
1 teaspoon sugar
1 tablespoon dry sherry

Rinse scallops and dry with paper towels.

Slice the baby corn in half lengthwise and remove ends from snow peas. Heat oil in a nonstick or well-seasoned wok and stir-fry shallots, garlic and ginger 1 minute.

Add scallops, baby corn and snow peas and stir-fry 1 minute. Stir in remaining ingredients and simmer 4 minutes or until scallops and vegetables are cooked through. Serve on a bed of rice.

Makes 4 servings.

Total Cals: 847	Total fat: 22.8 g
Cals per portion: 212	Fat per portion: 5.7 g

Note: Scallops are sometimes sold with edible orange roe still attached.

SHRIMP NOODLES

8 oz. vermicelli rice noodles
1 oz. dried Chinese mushrooms, soaked in hot water
    20 minutes
2 teaspoons chile oil
4 green onions, shredded
8 oz. cooked, peeled large shrimp, thawed and
    dried, if frozen
8 oz. frozen green peas
1 tablespoon oyster sauce
Grated zest of 1 lemon
1 egg, lightly beaten

Bring a large saucepan of water to a boil.
Turn off heat and add noodles. Loosen with
2 forks and let soak 3 minutes.

Drain noodles well and rinse in cold water.
Drain mushrooms and squeeze out excess
water. Discard stems and slice caps. Heat half
chile oil in a nonstick or well-seasoned wok
and stir-fry mushrooms, green onions,
shrimp and peas 2 minutes. Add oyster
sauce, lemon zest and noodles and stir-fry 2
minutes. Keep warm.

Heat remaining oil in a small nonstick skillet
and cook egg 1 or 2 minutes on each side or
until set. Slide onto a plate, roll up and cut
into thin slices. Garnish noodles with egg and
serve immediately.

Makes 4 servings.

Total Cals: 1489   Total fat: 30.7 g
Cals per portion: 372   Fat per portion: 7.7 g

—CHICKEN WITH MUSHROOMS—

1 lb. skinless, boneless chicken thighs
1 tablespoon sunflower oil
8 oz. button mushrooms, sliced
8 oz. green onions, chopped
1 garlic clove, finely chopped
1-inch piece fresh ginger root, peeled and finely chopped
2/3 cup Chinese Chicken Stock, page 12
2 tablespoons rice wine
2 tablespoons dark soy sauce
2 tablespoons oyster sauce
1 (15-oz.) can straw mushrooms, drained
1 teaspoon cornstarch mixed with 2 teaspoons water

Trim fat from chicken thighs. Cut meat into 1-inch strips. Heat oil in a nonstick or well-seasoned wok and stir-fry chicken strips 3 or 4 minutes or until chicken is lightly browned all over.

Add sliced mushrooms, green onions, garlic and ginger and stir-fry 2 minutes. Stir in remaining ingredients and simmer, stirring, 5 minutes. Serve with noodles.

Makes 4 servings.

Total Cals: 893   Total fat: 39.6 g
Cals per portion: 223   Fat per portion: 9.9 g

── GINGER CHICKEN PATTIES ──

1 lb. lean ground chicken
1 garlic clove, finely chopped
1-inch piece fresh ginger root, peeled and finely
    chopped
1/4 cup chopped fresh cilantro
1 tablespoon cornstarch
2 cups cooked long-grain white rice
Salt and freshly ground pepper
1 egg white, lightly beaten
2 teaspoons sunflower oil
Fresh cilantro leaves, to garnish
DIP:
2 tablespoons light soy sauce
2 tablespoons dry sherry
1/2-inch piece fresh ginger root, peeled and grated

In a bowl, mix together chicken, garlic, ginger and cilantro. Stir in cornstarch, rice, salt and pepper. Stir in egg white. Divide mixture into 8 portions and shape into 3-inch diameter patties, dusting the hands with extra cornstarch if needed. Place on a plate, cover and chill 30 minutes.

Preheat broiler. Brush broiler rack lightly with oil and place patties on rack. Brush tops lightly with oil and cook 4 minutes. Turn patties over, brush again with oil and cook another 3 or 4 minutes or until cooked through. Drain on paper towels. Mix together ingredients dip. Garnish patties with cilantro and serve with dip and a salad.

Makes 4 servings.

Total Cals: 1048   Total fat: 33.2 g
Cals per portion: 262   Fat per portion: 8.3 g

— CHICKEN & BASIL STIR-FRY —

1 lb. boneless chicken thighs
1 tablespoon dark soy sauce
1 tablespoon cornstarch
1 tablespoon peanut oil
2 garlic cloves, thinly sliced
1 fresh red chile, seeded and thinly sliced
1 teaspoon chile powder
1 tablespoon hoisin sauce
Small bunch basil leaves, shredded
Basil leaves and blanched red chile strips, to garnish

Remove skin and fat from chicken. Cut meat into 1-inch strips and place in a bowl. Stir in soy sauce and cornstarch.

Heat oil in a nonstick or well-seasoned wok and stir-fry chicken with garlic and chile 7 or 8 minutes.

Add chile powder and hoisin sauce and cook another 2 minutes. Remove from heat and stir in shredded basil. Garnish with basil leaves and chile strips and serve on a bed of rice.

Makes 4 servings.

Total Cals: 720   Total fat: 37.2 g
Cals per portion: 178   Fat per portion: 9.3 g

—LEMON & HONEY CHICKEN—

4 boneless chicken breasts, each weighing 4 oz.
3 tablespoons honey
4 teaspoons light soy sauce
Grated zest and juice of 2 lemons
1 garlic clove, finely chopped
Freshly ground pepper
1 tablespoon sunflower oil
2 tablespoons chopped fresh chives
Thin strips of lemon zest, to garnish

Remove skin and fat from chicken breasts. Using a sharp knife, score chicken breasts in a crisscross pattern on both sides, taking care not to slice all way through. Place in a shallow dish.

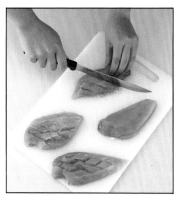

Mix together honey, soy sauce, lemon zest and juice, garlic and pepper. Pour over chicken, cover and chill 1 hour.

Heat oil in a nonstick or well-seasoned wok. Drain chicken, reserving marinade, and cook 2 or 3 minutes on each side, until lightly golden. Add marinade and simmer 5 minutes, turning frequently, until chicken is cooked through and sauce syrupy. Stir in chives, garnish with lemon zest and serve on a bed of noodles.

Makes 4 servings.

Total Cals: 814
Cals per portion: 204

Total fat: 27.6 g
Fat per portion: 6.9 g

───── CHICKEN CHOW MEIN ─────

8 oz. dried egg noodles
8 oz. skinless, boneless chicken breasts
1 tablespoon light soy sauce
1 tablespoon dry sherry
1 tablespoon sunflower oil
4 shallots, finely chopped
4 oz. snow peas, sliced diagonally
1 oz. Prosciutto, trimmed and finely diced
1 teaspoon sesame oil
1 teaspoon sugar
2 green onions, finely shredded, to garnish

Bring a large saucepan of water to a boil and cook noodles 3 or 4 minutes. Drain well, rinse, put in cold water and set aside. Trim chicken breasts. Using a sharp knife, shred into 1/4-inch strips. In a bowl, mix chicken strips with soy sauce and sherry.

Heat sunflower oil in a nonstick or well-seasoned wok and stir-fry chicken and shallots 2 minutes. Add snow peas and ham and stir-fry 1 minute. Drain noodles well and add to pan along with sesame oil and sugar. Cook, stirring, 2 minutes to warm through. Garnish with green onions and serve.

Makes 4 servings.

Total Cals: 1586   Total fat: 56.3 g
Cals per portion: 397   Fat per portion: 14.07 g

—CHICKEN & PLUM CASSEROLE—

1 oz. dried Chinese mushrooms, soaked in hot water
  20 minutes
1 lb. skinless, boneless chicken thighs
1 tablespoon sunflower oil
2 garlic cloves, thinly sliced
1 oz. Prosciutto, trimmed and diced
8 oz. plums, halved and pitted
1 tablespoon brown sugar
3 tablespoons light soy sauce
2 tablespoons rice wine
3 tablespoons plum sauce
1 tablespoon chile sauce
2-1/2 cups Chinese Chicken Stock, page 12
2 teaspoons cornstarch mixed with 4 teaspoons
  water

Drain mushrooms and squeeze out excess
water. Discard mushroom stems and thinly
slice caps. Trim fat from chicken thighs and
cut meat into 1-inch strips. Heat oil in a
nonstick or well-seasoned wok and stir-fry
chicken, garlic and ham 3 or 4 minutes. Add
mushrooms and stir-fry 1 minute.

Add remaining ingredients except cornstarch
mixture and simmer 20 minutes or until
plums have softened. Add cornstarch
mixture, and cook, stirring, until thickened.
Serve on a bed of rice.

Makes 4 servings.

Total Cals: 1375   Total fat: 54.9 g
Cals per portion: 339   Fat per portion: 13.72 g

——CHICKEN WITH PEANUTS——

1 lb. boneless chicken breasts
1 tablespoon chile oil
1-inch piece fresh ginger root, peeled and finely
  chopped
2 oz. peanuts, skins removed
1 tablespoon Chinese Chicken Stock, page 12
1 tablespoon dry sherry
1 tablespoon dark soy sauce
1 teaspoon brown sugar
1 teaspoon five-spice powder
1 teaspoon white rice vinegar
4 green onions, finely chopped

Remove skin and fat from chicken breasts.
Cut into 1-inch pieces.

Heat oil in a nonstick or well-seasoned wok
and gently stir-fry chicken, ginger and
peanuts 2 minutes or until chicken is just
colored.

Add remaining ingredients except the green
onions and simmer 5 minutes, stirring
occasionally. Remove from heat and stir in
green onions. Serve with a salad.

Makes 4 servings.

Total Cals: 982   Total fat: 45.3 g
Cals per portion: 246   Fat per portion: 11.32 g

—CHICKEN WITH CUCUMBER—

8 oz. cucumber
2 teaspoons salt
1 lb. boneless chicken breasts
1 tablespoon peanut oil
2 garlic cloves, finely chopped
1 tablespoon light soy sauce
1 tablespoon dry sherry
2 tablespoons chopped fresh chives
Cucumber twists, to garnish

Peel cucumber, halve lengthwise and scoop out the seeds with a teaspoon. Cut into 1-inch cubes, place in a bowl and sprinkle with salt. Set aside 20 minutes.

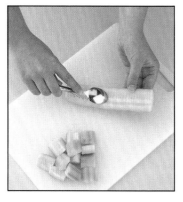

Remove skin and fat from chicken. Cut into 1/2-inch strips. Drain cucumber and rinse well. Pat dry with paper towels.

Heat oil in a nonstick or well-seasoned wok and stir-fry chicken and garlic 5 minutes. Add soy sauce, sherry, chives and cucumber and cook 3 minutes. Garnish with cucumber twists and serve with noodles.

Makes 4 servings.

Total Cals: 657   Total fat: 27.7 g
Cals per portion: 164   Fat per portion: 6.93 g

— PEPPERED CHICKEN KEBABS —

1 lb. skinless, boneless chicken breasts, cubed
1 tablespoon rice wine
1 tablespoon dark soy sauce
Grated zest and juice of 1 lime
2 teaspoons brown sugar
1 teaspoon ground cinnamon
1 teaspoon sunflower oil
1 teaspoon Szechuan peppercorns, toasted and
   crushed
Strips of lime zest, to garnish

Place chicken in a shallow dish. Mix together rice wine, soy sauce, lime zest and juice, sugar and cinnamon. Pour over chicken.

Cover chicken and chill 1 hour. Meanwhile, soak 8 bamboo skewers in cold water 30 minutes. Remove chicken pieces from marinade, reserving marinade, and thread chicken on to skewers.

Preheat broiler. Brush broiler rack lightly with oil and place skewers on rack. Brush with marinade and sprinkle with peppercorns. Broil 3 minutes, turn, brush again and broil another 2 or 3 minutes or until cooked through. Drain on paper towels. Garnish with lime zest and serve with wedges of lime and shredded napa cabbage.

Makes 4 servings.

Total Cals: 562   Total fat: 13.2 g
Cals per portion: 140   Fat per portion: 3.3 g

— CHINESE BARBECUE CHICKEN —

4 chicken quarters, each weighing 8 oz.
2 garlic cloves, finely chopped
1-inch piece fresh ginger root, peeled and finely
**   chopped**
1/4 cup hoisin sauce
2 tablespoons dry sherry
1 teaspoon chile sauce
1 tablespoon dark soy sauce
1 tablespoon brown sugar
1 tablespoon chopped fresh chives, to garnish

Remove skin and fat from chicken quarters. Rinse and pat dry with paper towels. Using a sharp knife, score the top of the quarters in diagonal lines.

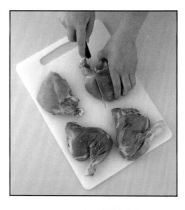

Place chicken in a shallow dish. Mix together all the remaining ingredients except the chives and spoon over the prepared quarters. Cover and chill overnight.

Preheat broiler or grill. Place chicken on broiler rack and cook 20 minutes, turning once, until cooked through. Garnish with chives and serve with rice and salad.

Makes 4 servings.

Total Cals: 673   Total fat: 18.7 g
Cals per portion: 168   Fat per portion: 4.68 g

——— DUCK WITH KIWI FRUIT ———

2 boneless duck breasts, each weighing 8 oz.
1/2-inch piece fresh ginger root, peeled and finely
   chopped
1 garlic clove, finely chopped
2 tablespoons dry sherry
2 kiwi fruit
1 teaspoon sesame oil
SAUCE:
1/4 cup dry sherry
2 tablespoons light soy sauce
4 teaspoons honey

Remove skin and fat from duck breasts.
With a sharp knife, score flesh in diagonal
lines. Beat with a meat tenderizer until
1/2-inch thick.

Place duck breasts in a shallow dish and add
ginger, garlic and sherry. Cover and chill 1
hour. Peel and thinly slice kiwi fruit and
halve crosswise. Cover and chill until
required. Preheat broiler. Drain duck breasts
and place on broiler rack. Brush with sesame
oil and cook 8 minutes. Turn and brush
again with oil. Cook 8 to 10 minutes until
tender and cooked through.

Meanwhile, put the sauce ingredients in a
saucepan, bring to a boil and simmer 5
minutes or until syrupy. Drain duck breasts
on paper towels and slice thinly. Arrange
duck slices and kiwi fruit on serving plates.
Pour sauce over duck and serve with rice and
vegetables.

Makes 4 servings.

Total Cals: 825   Total fat: 24.6 g
Cals per portion: 206   Fat per portion: 6.15 g

—— SOY-ROASTED DUCKLING ——

1 (5-lb.) duckling, giblets removed
1/4 cup dark soy sauce
2 tablespoons brown sugar
2 garlic cloves, finely chopped
DIP:
1 tablespoon sunflower oil
4 green onions, finely chopped
1 garlic clove, finely chopped
3 tablespoons dark soy sauce
2 teaspoons brown sugar
2 tablespoons dry sherry

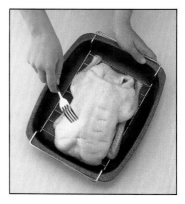

Preheat oven to 375F (190C). Rinse duckling and pat dry. Place on a wire rack in a roasting pan. Prick all over with a fork.

Sprinkle duck with soy sauce, brown sugar and garlic. Bake 2 hours 15 minutes or until juices run clear and skin is well browned. Combine ingredients for dip. Heat oil in a nonstick or well-seasoned wok and stir-fry green onions and garlic 1 minute. Drain on paper towels and mix with remaining ingredients.

To serve, remove all skin and fat from duckling and shred flesh away from bone. Serve with the dip, soft pancakes and shredded green onions and cucumber.

Makes 4 servings.

Total Cals: 1248   Total fat: 47.8 g
Cals per portion: 312   Fat per portion: 11.95 g

Note: Soft pancakes can be bought ready-made from Chinese supermarkets.

──── SZECHUAN TURKEY ────

1 lb. lean boneless turkey
1 egg white, lightly beaten
Large pinch of salt
1 teaspoon cornstarch
1 tablespoon sunflower oil
1/2 teaspoon Szechuan peppercorns, toasted and
   crushed
8 oz. vegetable chow-chow, shredded
8 oz. snow peas
1 (4-oz.) can water chestnuts, rinsed and sliced

Remove skin and fat from turkey. Cut into
thin strips about 1/4-inch thick.

Place turkey strips in a bowl and mix with
egg white, salt and cornstarch. Cover and
chill 30 minutes.

Heat oil in a nonstick or well-seasoned wok
and stir-fry turkey with crushed peppercorns
2 minutes or until turkey is just colored. Add
remaining ingredients and stir-fry 3 minutes
or until just cooked through. Serve
immediately.

Makes 4 servings.

Total Cals: 757   Total fat: 20.8 g
Cals per portion: 189   Fat per portion: 5.2 g

SWEET & SOUR TURKEY

1 lb. lean skinless, boneless turkey
1 tablespoon sunflower oil
2 shallots, chopped
2 stalks celery, sliced
2 tablespoons light soy sauce
1 red bell pepper, sliced
1 yellow bell pepper, sliced
1 green bell pepper, sliced
1 (4-oz.) can bamboo shoots, drained
3 tablespoons plum sauce
2 tablespoons white rice vinegar
1 teaspoon sesame oil
2 tablespoons sesame seeds

Trim away any excess fat from turkey. Cut into 1-inch cubes. Heat oil in a nonstick or well-seasoned wok and stir-fry turkey, shallots and celery 2 or 3 minutes or until lightly colored.

Add soy sauce and bell peppers and stir-fry 2 minutes. Stir in bamboo shoots, plum sauce and vinegar and simmer 2 minutes. Stir in sesame oil, sprinkle with sesame seeds and serve.

Makes 4 servings.

Total Cals: 931
Cals per portion: 233

Total fat: 39 g
Fat per portion: 9.75 g

—TURKEY & BAMBOO CURRY—

3 tablespoons unsweetened shredded coconut,
    soaked in 2/3 cup boiling water 30 minutes
1 lb. lean skinless, boneless turkey
1 tablespoon sunflower oil
1 garlic clove, finely chopped
1/2-inch piece fresh ginger root, peeled and finely
    chopped
4 green onions, chopped
6 oz. baby corn
2 tablespoons dark soy sauce
1 whole cinnamon stick, broken
1 teaspoon ground coriander
2/3 cup Chinese Chicken Stock, page 12
1 (4-oz.) can bamboo shoots, drained

Pour coconut mixture through a fine strainer
placed over a bowl, pressing the coconut
with the back of a spoon to extract all the
liquid. Reserve liquid and discard coconut.
Trim away any excess fat from turkey. Cut
into 1/2-inch strips. Heat oil in a nonstick or
well-seasoned wok and stir-fry turkey, garlic,
ginger, green onions and baby corn 2 minutes
or until turkey is lightly colored.

Stir in soy sauce, cinnamon stick, ground
coriander, coconut water and stock. Bring to
a boil and simmer 20 minutes. Stir in
bamboo shoots and simmer 5 minutes.
Discard cinnamon stick and serve with rice
and salad.

Makes 4 servings.

Total Cals: 849   Total fat: 38.2 g
Cals per portion: 212   Fat per portion: 9.55 g

—— CILANTRO TURKEY RICE ——

1 tablespoon sunflower oil
2 shallots, chopped
2 garlic cloves, finely chopped
1 oz. Prosciutto, trimmed and cut into strips
1-1/4 cups long-grain white rice, rinsed
1 teaspoon ground coriander
Salt and freshly ground pepper
3-3/4 cups Chinese Chicken Stock, page 12
4 oz. asparagus, cut into 1-inch pieces, blanched
1 (8-oz.) package frozen green peas
8 oz. cooked turkey, skinned and diced
1/4 cup chopped fresh cilantro

Heat oil in a nonstick or well-seasoned wok and stir-fry shallots, garlic, ham, rice and ground coriander 2 minutes. Season with salt and pepper.

Pour in stock and bring to a boil. Reduce heat and simmer 20 minutes. Gently stir in asparagus, peas, turkey and cilantro and cook over low heat 5 minutes or until heated through, stirring to prevent sticking. Serve immediately.

Makes 4 servings.

Total Cals: 1954   Total fat: 37.6 g
Cals per portion: 489   Fat per portion: 9.4 g

–GINGER BEEF WITH PINEAPPLE–

1 lb. lean beef round or sirloin steak
Salt and freshly ground pepper
1 tablespoon sweet sherry
1-inch piece fresh ginger root, peeled and finely
  chopped
1 garlic clove, finely chopped
1 teaspoon cornstarch
8 oz. fresh pineapple
1 tablespoon sunflower oil
2 red bell peppers, thinly sliced
4 green onions, chopped
2 tablespoons light soy sauce
1 piece stem ginger in syrup, drained and thinly
  sliced

Trim any visible fat from the beef and cut into 1/4-inch strips. Place in a bowl and season. Add sherry, chopped ginger, garlic and cornstarch and mix well. Cover and chill 30 minutes. Meanwhile, peel and core the pineapple and cut into 1-inch cubes.

Heat oil in a nonstick or well-seasoned wok, add beef mixture and stir-fry 1 or 2 minutes or until beef is browned all over. Add bell peppers and stir-fry for another minute. Add green onions, pineapple and soy sauce and simmer 2 or 3 minutes, to heat through. Sprinkle with stem ginger and serve on a bed of noodles.

Makes 4 servings.

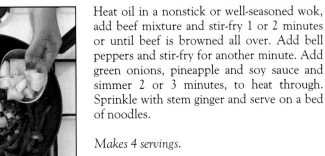

Total Cals: 943	Total fat: 36.9 g
Cals per portion: 236	Fat per portion: 9.2 g

—STEAKS WITH CHILE SAUCE—

4 lean beef fillets, each weighing 4 oz.
1 teaspoon dark soy sauce
1 garlic clove, finely chopped
1 teaspoon sesame oil
2 tablespoons chopped fresh chives, to garnish
SAUCE:
1 teaspoon sunflower oil
1 fresh green chile, seeded and finely chopped
1 shallot, finely chopped
1 teaspoon chile sauce
2 tablespoons red rice vinegar
1/4 cup dry sherry
1 teaspoon brown sugar

Trim any fat from steaks. Tenderize lightly with a meat tenderizer or rolling pin.

Preheat broiler. Place steaks on broiler rack. Mix together soy sauce, garlic and sesame oil and brush over steaks. Broil 3 or 4 minutes on each side, brushing with the soy sauce mixture to prevent drying out.

Meanwhile, make the sauce. Heat oil in a nonstick or well-seasoned wok and stir-fry the chile and shallot over a low heat 1 minute. Add remaining ingredients and simmer 2 or 3 minutes. Drain cooked steaks on paper towels. Sprinkle with chives and serve with the sauce and a salad.

Makes 4 servings.

Total Cals: 743
Cals per portion: 186

Total fat: 30.8 g
Fat per portion: 7.7 g

—MANGO BEEF WITH CASHEWS—

1 lb. lean beef round or sirloin steak
1 garlic clove, finely chopped
1 tablespoon light soy sauce
1 tablespoon rice wine
1 teaspoon cornstarch
Salt and freshly ground pepper
2 ripe mangoes
1 tablespoon sunflower oil
2 tablespoons chopped fresh cilantro
1 oz. unsalted cashew nuts, coarsely crushed

Trim any fat from the beef and cut into 1/4-inch strips.

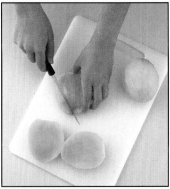

Place in a bowl and mix with garlic, soy sauce, rice wine, cornstarch, salt and pepper. Cover and chill 30 minutes. Peel the mangoes and slice flesh off the large flat pit in the center of each mango. Cut flesh into thick, even slices, reserving a few small strips garnish.

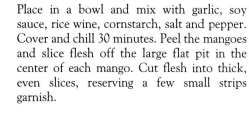

Heat oil in a nonstick or well-seasoned wok and stir-fry beef mixture 3 or 4 minutes until beef is browned all over. Stir in sliced mango and cook over low heat 2 or 3 minutes to heat through. Sprinkle with chopped cilantro and crushed cashews, garnish with reserved mango and serve on a bed of rice.

Makes 4 servings.

Total Cals: 1149   Total fat: 50.2 g
Cals per portion: 287   Fat per portion: 12.55 g

ROAST HOISIN BEEF

1 (1-1/2-lb.) lean beef top round roast
Freshly ground pepper
2 garlic cloves, finely chopped
1/2-inch piece fresh ginger root, peeled and finely
    chopped
2 teaspoons sesame oil
1/4 cup hoisin sauce
2 cups Chinese Beef Stock, page 13
4 carrots
1 daikon
1 large green bell pepper
1 large yellow bell pepper
4 green onions, shredded
Green onion rings, to garnish

Preheat oven to 350F (175C). Trim any fat from the beef and place in a nonstick roasting pan. Season with pepper. Mix together garlic, ginger, sesame oil and hoisin sauce and spread over beef. Pour half the stock into the pan and roast 1 hour, basting occasionally to prevent drying out.

Meanwhile, peel carrots and daikon. Halve carrots and slice lengthwise. Slice daikon crosswise. Quarter the bell peppers. Arrange vegetables around beef, pour in remaining stock and cook 45 to 60 minutes or until tender. Drain beef and vegetables. Slice beef and serve with vegetables, topped with shredded green onions and garnished with green onion rings.

Makes 4 servings.

Total Cals: 1429   Total fat: 48.4 g
Cals per portion: 357   Fat per portion: 12.1 g

—STIR-FRIED BEEF WITH LEEKS—

1 lb. lean beef round or sirloin steak
1 tablespoon dark soy sauce
1 teaspoon sesame oil
Freshly ground pepper
1 tablespoon dry sherry
2 teaspoons cornstarch
1 lb. leeks
4 oz. green onions
2 teaspoons sunflower oil
2 teaspoons sugar
2/3 cup Chinese Beef Stock, page 13
2 tablespoons chopped fresh chives
Fresh chives, to garnish

Trim any fat from the beef and cut into 3/4-inch pieces. Place in a bowl and mix in soy sauce, sesame oil, pepper, sherry and cornstarch. Cover and chill 30 minutes. Trim leeks and discard any coarse outer leaves. Slice thinly and wash well to remove any soil. Trim and shred green onions.

Heat oil in a nonstick or well-seasoned wok and stir-fry beef mixture 1 or 2 minutes or until beef is browned. Add leeks, green onions and sugar and stir-fry 3 or 4 minutes or until browned. Pour in stock and simmer 5 minutes, stirring occasionally, until thickened. Stir in chopped chives, garnish with chives and serve with noodles.

Makes 4 servings.

Total Cals: 955   Total fat: 38.3 g
Cals per portion: 239   Fat per portion: 9.6 g

GARLIC BEEF CASSEROLE

1 lb. lean beef chuck, trimmed and cut into 3/4-inch
  cubes
1 tablespoon peanut oil
2 shallots, chopped
4 garlic cloves, thinly sliced
2 large carrots, sliced
6 oz. baby corn, halved lengthwise
8 oz. button mushrooms
1-1/4 cups Chinese Beef Stock, page 13
2 tablespoons dark soy sauce
1 tablespoon rice wine
2 teaspoons five-spice powder
2 tablespoons hoisin sauce
1 teaspoon chile sauce

Heat oil in a nonstick or well-seasoned wok
and stir-fry beef, shallots, garlic, carrots,
baby corn and mushrooms 5 minutes. Add
remaining ingredients and bring to a boil.
Reduce to a simmer, cover and simmer 1
hour.

Remove from heat and blot surface with
paper towels to absorb surface fat. Increase
the heat and boil 10 minutes to reduce and
thicken sauce. Serve with rice.

Makes 4 servings.

Total Cals: 1021   Total fat: 39.1 g
Cals per portion: 255   Fat per portion: 9.8 g

─────── LIGHT BEEF SATAY ───────

1 lb. lean beef round or sirloin steak
MARINADE:
1 shallot, finely chopped
1-inch piece fresh ginger root, peeled and finely
   chopped
2 garlic cloves, finely chopped
Zest and juice of 1 lime
2 teaspoons garam masala
Salt and freshly ground pepper
1 teaspoon light soy sauce
SAUCE:
6 tablespoons unsweetened shredded coconut
2 tablespoons crunchy peanut butter
1 tablespoon brown sugar
1 teaspoon sunflower oil
2 garlic cloves, finely chopped
1 fresh red chile, seeded and chopped
1 tablespoon dark soy sauce
Strips of fresh red chile, to garnish

Soak 8 bamboo skewers in cold water to prevent the beef sticking to them. Trim any fat from the beef and cut into 1/4-inch strips. Place in a shallow dish.

Mix together the marinade ingredients and pour over the beef. Mix well, cover and chill 2 hours.

Meanwhile, make the sauce. Place shredded coconut in a bowl and pour 1 cup boiling water over coconut. Leave for 30 minutes. Place a fine strainer over a bowl and pour the mixture through the strainer, pressing the coconut with a spatula or spoon to extract all the water. Discard coconut.

Blend coconut water with the peanut butter and brown sugar. Heat oil in a nonstick or well-seasoned wok and stir-fry garlic and chile 1 minute. Stir in peanut butter mixture and soy sauce and bring to a boil. Reduce heat and simmer 10 minutes, stirring occasionally, until thickened. Set aside.

Thread beef strips along each skewer in the shape of an S. Preheat broiler. Cover ends of skewers with foil to prevent burning. Broil beef 3 or 4 minutes on each side. Drain on paper towels. Reheat peanut sauce. Garnish with strips of red chile. Serve skewers on a bed of rice with the peanut sauce, lime wedges and a green salad.

Makes 4 servings.

Total Cals: 973	Total fat: 48 g
Cals per portion: 243	Fat per portion: 12 g

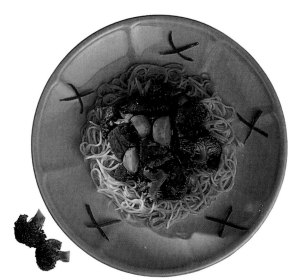

– BEEF WITH WATER CHESTNUTS –

1 lb. lean beef round or sirloin steak
1 tablespoon dark soy sauce
1 tablespoon dry sherry
1 teaspoon chile sauce
2 teaspoons brown sugar
2 teaspoons cornstarch
8 oz. broccoli
1 (4-oz.) can water chestnuts, drained
1 tablespoon sunflower oil
Salt and freshly ground pepper
Strips of fresh red chile, to garnish

Trim any fat from beef and cut into 3/4-inch pieces.

Place beef in a bowl, and mix with soy sauce, sherry, chile sauce, sugar and cornstarch. Cover and chill 30 minutes. Meanwhile, cut broccoli into small flowerets. Bring a small saucepan of water to a boil and cook broccoli 3 minutes. Drain and rinse in cold water. Halve water chestnuts.

Heat oil in a nonstick or well-seasoned wok. Add beef mixture and stir-fry 2 or 3 minutes. Add broccoli and water chestnuts, season with salt and pepper and stir-fry 3 minutes. Garnish with red chile strips and serve with noodles.

Makes 4 servings.

Total Cals: 898   Total fat: 37.9 g
Cals per portion: 224   Fat per portion: 9.5 g

SZECHUAN BEEF

1 lb. lean beef fillet
1 tablespoon sunflower oil
1 garlic clove, finely chopped
1/2-inch piece fresh ginger root, peeled and finely
  chopped
4 green onions, finely chopped
1 tablespoon hoisin sauce
1 teaspoon Szechuan peppercorns, toasted and
  ground
4 oz. vegetable chow-chow
1 teaspoon sugar
Shredded green onions, to garnish

Trim any fat and silver skin from beef. Cut beef into very thin slices.

Heat oil in a nonstick or well-seasoned wok and stir-fry beef, garlic, ginger and green onions 1 minute or until beef is browned.

Add remaining ingredients except the garnish and stir-fry 3 or 4 minutes or until beef is just cooked through. Garnish with shredded green onions and serve with rice.

Makes 4 servings.

Total Cals: 790   Total fat: 36.9 g
Cals per portion: 197   Fat per portion: 9.2 g

—STIR-FRIED CITRUS BEEF—

12 oz. lean beef round or sirloin steak
2 tablespoons dark soy sauce
1 tablespoon dry sherry
2 pieces preserved mandarin orange peel, shredded
Grated zest of 1 lime
Grated zest and juice of 1 orange
1 whole cinnamon stick, broken
2 teaspoons cornstarch
2 teaspoons sunflower oil
4 green onions, shredded
Freshly ground pepper
8 clusters vermicelli egg noodles, each weighing 1 oz.
Lime and orange slices and zest, to garnish

Trim any fat from the beef and cut beef into 3/4-inch pieces. Place in a bowl.

Add soy sauce, sherry, mandarin peel, lime zest, orange zest and juice, cinnamon stick and cornstarch and mix well. Cover and chill 30 minutes. Heat oil in a nonstick or well-seasoned wok and stir-fry beef mixture for 2 or 3 minutes. Add green onions and pepper and simmer 2 or 3 minutes or until beef is tender. Discard cinnamon.

Meanwhile, bring a large saucepan of water to a boil, add noodle clusters, reduce heat and simmer 2 or 3 minutes, taking care they retain their shape. Remove from pan with a slotted spoon, drain well and arrange on serving plates. Top with the beef mixture, garnish and serve with steamed carrots.

Makes 4 servings.

Total Cals: 1535   Total fat: 44.5 g
Cals per portion: 384   Fat per portion: 11.1 g

— STEAKS WITH SHERRY DIP —

4 lean beef fillets each weighing 4 oz.
Freshly ground pepper
1 tablespoon dry sherry
1-inch piece fresh ginger root, peeled and finely
   chopped
1 teaspoon sesame oil
4 green onions, finely chopped, and green onion
   strips, to garnish
DIP:
2 teaspoons sunflower oil
4 green onions, finely chopped
1/2-inch piece fresh ginger root, peeled and finely
   chopped
1/4 cup dry sherry
2 tablespoons dark soy sauce

Trim any fat and silver skin from the steaks
and lightly tenderize with a meat tenderizer.
Season both sides with pepper. Mix together
sherry, ginger and sesame oil. Preheat broiler.
Place steaks on broiler rack and brush with
the sherry mixture. Broil 3 or 4 minutes on
each side, basting to prevent drying out.
Drain on paper towels.

Meanwhile, make the dip. Heat oil in a
nonstick or well-seasoned wok and stir-fry
green onions and ginger 2 minutes or until
soft. Drain well on paper towels and place
in a bowl. Mix in sherry and soy sauce.
Garnish steaks with chopped green onions
and green onion flowers and serve with the
dip and a salad.

Makes 4 servings.

Total Cals: 864   Total fat: 35.7 g
Cals per portion: 216   Fat per portion: 8.9 g

—— BLACK-BEAN BEEF & RICE ——

1 tablespoon sunflower oil
2 shallots, chopped
2 garlic cloves, finely chopped
1 whole cinnamon stick, broken
2 star anise
8 oz. lean beef chuck, trimmed and cut into 3/4-inch
 cubes
3 tablespoons fermented black beans
1-1/4 cups long-grain white rice, rinsed
3-1/2 cups Chinese Beef Stock, page 13
Salt and freshly ground pepper
2 tablespoons chopped fresh chives, to garnish

Heat oil in a nonstick or well-seasoned wok and stir-fry shallots, garlic, cinnamon stick, star anise, beef, black beans and rice 2 or 3 minutes or until beef is browned and rice is opaque.

Pour in stock and bring to a boil. Reduce heat and simmer 25 minutes or until liquid is absorbed and beef is tender. Discard cinnamon stick and star anise. Garnish with chives and serve with a salad.

Makes 4 servings.

Total Cals: 1812   Total fat: 28.9 g
Cals per portion: 453   Fat per portion: 7.2 g

CURRIED BEEF

2 tablespoons light soy sauce
1/4 cup Madras curry paste
1 tablespoon rice wine
1 tablespoon brown sugar
1 tablespoon peanut oil
1 lb. lean beef round or sirloin steak, trimmed and
  cut into 3/4-inch cubes
8 oz. shallots, halved
2 garlic cloves, finely chopped
1-1/4 cups Chinese Beef Stock, page 13
1 teaspoon cornstarch mixed with 2 teaspoons water
Grated zest of 1 orange
1/4 cup chopped fresh cilantro
Orange segments, to garnish

Blend together soy sauce, curry paste, rice wine and sugar and set aside. Heat oil in a nonstick or well-seasoned wok and stir-fry beef, shallots and garlic 2 or 3 minutes or until browned. Add soy sauce mixture and stir-fry 1 minute. Pour in stock and bring to a boil. Reduce heat, cover and simmer 1 hour or until tender.

Skim any fat or scum from surface. Stir in cornstarch mixture, orange zest and half of the cilantro. Cook, stirring, 3 or 4 minutes until thickened. Sprinkle with remaining cilantro, garnish with orange segments and serve on a bed of rice.

Makes 4 servings.

Total Cals: 1229   Total fat: 48.2 g
Cals per portion: 307   Fat per portion: 12.05 g

— BEEF WITH OYSTER SAUCE —

1 lb. lean beef round or sirloin steak
1 oz. dried Chinese mushrooms, soaked in hot water
  20 minutes
8 oz. oyster mushrooms
1 tablespoon light soy sauce
1 tablespoon dry sherry
Freshly ground pepper
2 tablespoons oyster sauce
1 tablespoon sunflower oil
2 tablespoons chopped fresh chives, to garnish

Trim any fat from steak and cut into 1/4-inch strips. Drain soaked mushrooms, squeezing out excess water. Discard stems and slice caps. Slice oyster mushrooms.

Mix together soy sauce, sherry, pepper and oyster sauce and set aside. Heat oil in a nonstick or well-seasoned wok and stir-fry beef and mushrooms 2 or 3 minutes or until beef is browned.

Stir soy sauce mixture into beef and stir-fry 2 or 3 minutes or until beef is tender. Garnish with chives and serve on a bed of noodles with freshly cooked vegetables.

Makes 4 servings.

Total Cals: 865   Total fat: 36.9 g
Cals per portion: 216   Fat per portion: 9.2 g

SPINACH & PORK BALLS

8 oz. fresh spinach, large stems removed
4 green onions, finely chopped
12 oz. lean ground pork
1 garlic clove, finely chopped
1 egg white
2 tablespoons cornstarch
Salt and freshly ground pepper
DIP:
2 tablespoons light soy sauce
1 garlic clove, finely chopped
2 tablespoons dry sherry
1 teaspoon brown sugar

Cook spinach in boiling salted water a few seconds or until soft. Drain and rinse in cold water. Dry on paper towels and shred.

In a bowl, mix together the spinach, green onions, ground pork, garlic, egg white, cornstarch, salt and pepper. Stir into a dough-like mixture and divide into 16 portions. Roll each portion into a ball, flouring the hands with extra cornstarch to prevent sticking.

Bring a wok or large saucepan of water to a boil. Arrange pork balls on a layer of parchment paper in a steamer, put over water, cover and steam 8 to 10 minutes or until cooked through. Mix together dip ingredients. Serve the pork balls with the dip and steamed vegetables.

Makes 4 servings.

Total Cals: 819   Total fat: 26.4 g
Cals per portion: 205   Fat per portion: 6.6 g

- HAM & SHRIMP BEAN SPROUTS -

12 oz. bean sprouts
1 tablespoon sunflower oil
4 oz. lean ham, trimmed and diced
4 oz. cooked, peeled large shrimp, thawed and
    dried, if frozen
4 oz. green onions, finely chopped
1 green bell pepper, chopped
2 tablespoons light soy sauce
Salt and freshly ground pepper
2 tablespoons chopped fresh chives, to garnish

Bring a large saucepan of water to a boil and
cook bean sprouts a few seconds or until
soft. Drain bean sprouts and rinse in cold
water. Dry on paper towels.

Heat oil in a nonstick or well-seasoned wok
and stir-fry ham, shrimp, green onions and
bell pepper 2 or 3 minutes or until lightly
golden.

Add soy sauce, bean sprouts, salt and
pepper and stir-fry 2 minutes to heat
through. Garnish with chopped chives and
serve with rice.

Makes 4 servings.

Total Cals: 574   Total fat: 25.3 g
Cals per portion: 143   Fat per portion: 6.3 g

HOT SWEET PORK

12 oz. lean pork fillet
1 tablespoon light soy sauce
1 tablespoon rice wine
Freshly ground pepper
1 tablespoon cornstarch
1 tablespoon sunflower oil
2 fresh red chiles, seeded and chopped
1 garlic clove, finely chopped
1 red bell pepper, diced
8 oz. zucchini, diced
1 (4-oz.) can bamboo shoots, drained
2 tablespoons red rice vinegar
2 tablespoons brown sugar
Large pinch of salt
1 tablespoon sesame seeds
Strips of fresh red chile, to garnish

Trim any fat and silver skin from pork fillet. Cut into 1/2-inch strips. Place in a bowl and mix with soy sauce, rice wine, pepper and cornstarch. Cover and chill 30 minutes.

Heat oil in a nonstick or well-seasoned wok and stir-fry pork mixture 1 or 2 minutes until pork is browned. Add remaining ingredients except the sesame seeds and garnish and stir-fry 4 or 5 minutes until vegetables are just cooked through. Sprinkle with sesame seeds, garnish with chile strips and serve with noodles.

Makes 4 servings.

Total Cals: 1007   Total fat: 47 g
Cals per portion: 252   Fat per portion: 11.75 g

——— POT-STICKER DUMPLINGS ———

1 cup all-purpose flour
1 tablespoon sunflower oil
FILLING:
4 oz. lean ground pork
1/2-inch piece fresh ginger root, peeled and finely
    chopped
1 tablespoon dark soy sauce
1 tablespoon dry sherry
Large pinch of ground white pepper

Place flour in a bowl and gradually add 1/2
cup hot water, mixing well to form a dough.
Turn out on to a floured surface and knead
until smooth.

Return to the bowl, cover and set aside 20
minutes. Mix together all filling ingredients.
Divide dough into 16 portions and, on a
floured surface, flatten each portion into a
2-1/2-inch diameter round. Take one round
at a time, keeping remaining rounds covered
with a damp dish towel, and place a little
filling in the center. Brush edge of dough
with water and bring together over the filling,
pinching edges together and pleating or
folding them to seal. Cover with a damp dish
towel while you make the remainder.

Heat oil in a nonstick or well-seasoned wok
and place dumplings, flat side down, in the
wok. Cook for 2 minutes until lightly
browned on bottom. Add 2/3 cups water,
cover and cook for 10 minutes. Uncover and
cook for 2 minutes. Drain and serve with a
crisp salad and hoisin sauce as a dip, if liked.

Makes 4 servings.

Total Cals: 728   Total fat: 24.5 g
Cals per portion: 182   Fat per portion: 6.1 g

──ROAST PORK WITH HONEY──

1 (1-lb.) piece lean pork fillet
1/4 cup chopped fresh cilantro
GLAZE:
1 teaspoon Szechuan peppercorns, toasted and
   ground
1 tablespoon honey
2 teaspoons brown sugar
1 tablespoon dark soy sauce
1-inch piece fresh ginger root, peeled and finely
   chopped
1 garlic clove, finely chopped

Preheat oven to 375F (190C). Trim any fat
and silver skin from pork and place fillet on a
rack in a roasting pan. Pour in enough water
to cover bottom of pan.

Mix together all ingredients glaze and brush
generously over pork. Roast 1 hour or until
cooked through, brushing occasionally with
glaze and adding more water to pan if it
dries out.

Remove cooked pork from rack and sprinkle
with chopped cilantro until coated all over.
Slice and serve with rice and vegetables.

Makes 4 servings.

Total Cals: 809   Total fat: 32.4 g
Cals per portion: 202   Fat per portion: 8.1 g

– BROILED CITRUS PORK CHOPS –

4 lean pork chops, trimmed, each weighing 4 oz.
Grated zest and juice of 1 lime, 1 small lemon and
1 small orange
1 teaspoon sesame oil
2 tablespoons dry sherry
2 tablespoons light soy sauce
1 tablespoon sugar
Large pinch of ground white pepper
1 teaspoon cornstarch mixed with 2 teaspoons water
Lime, lemon and orange slices and strips of zest, to
garnish

Score the chops in a crisscross pattern. Place in a shallow dish, sprinkle with citrus zests and top with juices.

Cover and chill 30 minutes. Drain chops well, reserving juices. Preheat broiler. Place chops on broiler rack and brush lightly with sesame oil. Broil 3 or 4 minutes on each side or until cooked through. Drain on paper towels and keep warm. Place reserved juices in a small saucepan with the remaining ingredients except the garnish. Bring to a boil, stirring until thickened.

Slice pork chops and arrange on serving plates with lime, lemon and orange slices. Top with sauce, garnish with strips of citrus zest and serve with a crisp salad.

Makes 4 servings.

Total Cals: 902   Total fat: 37.3 g
Cals per portion: 225   Fat per portion: 9.3 g

—— PORK WITH WALNUTS ——

1 lb. lean pork fillet
1 tablespoon rice wine
1 tablespoon light soy sauce
1 teaspoon cornstarch
1 bunch green onions
2 teaspoons sunflower oil
1 teaspoon sugar
Salt and freshly ground pepper
1 oz. walnut pieces

Trim any fat and silver skin from pork and cut fillet into 1/4-inch strips. Place in a bowl and add rice wine, soy sauce and cornstarch. Mix well, cover and chill 30 minutes.

Trim green onions, discarding any damaged outer leaves. Cut green onions into 2-inch pieces.

Heat oil in a nonstick or well-seasoned wok and stir-fry pork mixture 2 or 3 minutes or until browned. Add green onions, sugar, salt and pepper and stir-fry 3 minutes. Sprinkle with walnut pieces and serve with noodles.

Makes 4 servings.

Total Cals: 1056   Total fat: 51.2 g
Cals per portion: 264   Fat per portion: 12.8 g

———DRY PORK CURRY———

12 oz. lean boneless pork, trimmed and cut into
 3/4-inch cubes
1 tablespoon light brown sugar
12 oz. potatoes
8 oz. carrots
8 oz. shallots
1 tablespoon sunflower oil
1-inch piece fresh ginger root, peeled and finely
 chopped
2 tablespoons Madras curry paste
2/3 cup coconut milk
1-1/4 cups Chinese Chicken Stock, page 12
Salt and freshly ground pepper
2 tablespoons chopped fresh cilantro

In a bowl, mix together pork and brown
sugar and set aside. Cut potatoes and carrots
into 3/4-inch chunks. Peel and halve shallots.

Heat oil in a nonstick or well-seasoned wok
and stir-fry pork, ginger and vegetables 2 or 3
minutes or until lightly browned. Blend
curry paste with coconut milk, stock, salt
and pepper. Stir into pork mixture and bring
to a boil. Reduce heat and simmer 40
minutes. Sprinkle with cilantro and serve on
a bed of rice.

Makes 4 servings.

Total Cals: 1422   Total fat: 65 g
Cals per portion: 355   Fat per portion: 16.2 g

──STIR-FRIED SESAME LAMB──

12 oz. lean lamb fillet
1 tablespoon sunflower oil
4 oz. shallots, sliced
1 red bell pepper, sliced
1 green bell pepper, sliced
1 garlic clove, finely chopped
1 tablespoon light soy sauce
1 teaspoon white rice vinegar
1 teaspoon sugar
Freshly ground pepper
2 tablespoons sesame seeds

Trim any fat and silver skin from lamb fillet. Cut fillet into 1/4-inch cubes.

Heat oil in a nonstick or well-seasoned wok and stir-fry lamb 1 or 2 minutes or until browned. Remove with a slotted spoon and set aside. Stir-fry shallots, bell peppers and garlic 2 minutes or until just soft.

Return lamb to wok with all the remaining ingredients except the sesame seeds. Stir-fry 2 minutes. Sprinkle with sesame seeds and serve with rice and vegetables.

Makes 4 servings.

Total Cals: 922   Total fat: 58.5 g
Cals per portion: 230   Fat per portion: 14.6 g

—RED-COOKED LAMB FILLET—

1 lb. lean lamb fillet
3 tablespoons dry sherry
1/2-inch piece fresh ginger root, peeled and finely
   chopped
2 garlic cloves, thinly sliced
1 teaspoon five-spice powder
3 tablespoons dark soy sauce
1-1/4 cups Chinese Vegetable Stock, page 14
2 teaspoons sugar
2 teaspoons cornstarch mixed with 4 teaspoons
   water
Salt and freshly ground pepper
Shredded green onions, to garnish

Trim any excess fat and silver skin from lamb
and cut lamb into 3/4-inch cubes.

Cook lamb in a saucepan of boiling water
3 minutes. Drain well. Heat a nonstick or
well-seasoned wok and add lamb, sherry,
ginger, garlic, five-spice powder and soy
sauce. Bring to a boil, reduce heat and
simmer 2 minutes, stirring. Pour in stock,
return to a boil, then simmer 25 minutes.

Add sugar, cornstarch mixture, salt and
pepper and stir until thickened. Simmer 5
minutes. Garnish with shredded green
onions and serve on a bed of rice.

Makes 4 servings.

Total Cals: 931   Total fat: 40.2 g
Cals per portion: 233   Fat per portion: 10.05 g

STIR-FRIED MEATBALLS

1 (1-lb.) eggplant
1/4 cup salt
1 tablespoon sunflower oil
2 tablespoons rice wine
1 (4-oz.) can bamboo shoots, drained and cut into
    strips
4 green onions, finely chopped, to garnish
MEATBALLS:
12 oz. lean ground lamb
4 green onions, finely chopped
2 garlic cloves, finely chopped
2 tablespoons chopped fresh chives
Salt and ground white pepper
1 teaspoon ground cinnamon
2 teaspoons cornstarch
1 egg white

Cut eggplant into 1/4-inch slices and layer in a bowl, sprinkling generously with salt. Set aside 30 minutes. Meanwhile, mix together meatball ingredients. Divide mixture into 24 portions and roll into balls, flouring the hands with extra cornstarch. Set aside. Transfer eggplant to a colander and rinse well under cold running water, pressing gently to remove all salt and bitterness. Drain well and pat dry with paper towels.

Heat oil and rice wine in a nonstick or well-seasoned wok and stir-fry eggplant 2 or 3 minutes or until softened. Add meatballs and carefully stir-fry 5 minutes. Add bamboo shoots and stir-fry 2 minutes. Remove meatballs and vegetables with a slotted spoon. Garnish with chopped green onions and serve with a salad.

Makes 4 servings.

Total Cals: 906   Total fat: 47.1 g
Cals per portion: 226   Fat per portion: 11.8 g

YELLOW BEAN LAMB

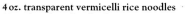

4 oz. transparent vermicelli rice noodles
12 oz. lean boneless lamb
1 tablespoon peanut oil
1 garlic clove, finely chopped
2 green onions, finely chopped
4 oz. snow peas, sliced
2 tablespoons yellow bean sauce
Freshly ground pepper
2 tablespoons chopped fresh chives, to garnish

Bring a saucepan of water to a boil. Remove from heat and add noodles. Leave to soak 2 or 3 minutes or until soft, then drain well and set aside.

Trim any fat from the lamb and cut into 1/2-inch strips. Heat oil in a nonstick or well-seasoned wok and stir-fry lamb, garlic, green onions and snow peas 2 or 3 minutes or until lamb is browned.

Stir in yellow bean sauce and noodles, season with pepper and stir-fry 3 minutes. Garnish with chopped chives and serve with a mixed salad.

Makes 4 servings.

Total Cals: 1223   Total fat: 52.3 g
Cals per portion: 306   Fat per portion: 13.1 g

LAMB WITH STAR ANISE

4 lean lamb loin chops, each weighing 5 oz.
2 teaspoons sunflower oil
1 garlic clove, thinly sliced
4 star anise
1 tablespoon light soy sauce
1/4 cup dry sherry
1 teaspoon sugar
Salt and ground white pepper
1 teaspoon cornstarch mixed with 2 teaspoons water
2 green onions, shredded, to garnish

Trim fat and bone from the lamb. Using string, tie lamb into rounds.

Heat oil in a nonstick or well-seasoned wok, add garlic and lamb and fry 2 minutes on each side until browned. Drain on paper towels and wipe out wok. Return lamb and garlic to wok. Add star anise, soy sauce, sherry, sugar, salt and pepper.

Bring to a boil, reduce heat and simmer 4 minutes, turning lamb halfway through. Add cornstarch mixture and cook, stirring, until thickened. Simmer 2 minutes. Discard star anise and remove string from lamb before serving. Garnish with green onions and serve with rice and vegetables.

Makes 4 servings.

Total Cals: 961   Total fat: 50 g
Cals per portion: 240   Fat per portion: 12.5 g

CILANTRO CHICKEN

2 teaspoons sunflower oil
1 garlic clove, finely chopped
1 shallot, finely chopped
12 oz. lean cooked skinless chicken, diced
1 teaspoon ground coriander
2 teaspoons dark soy sauce
Freshly ground pepper
2 tablespoons chopped fresh cilantro
4 oz. bean sprouts
1 large carrot, grated
1 oz. fresh cilantro leaves
2 nectarines, sliced
2 bananas, halved, sliced and tossed in juice of
    1 small lemon

Heat oil in a nonstick or well-seasoned wok and stir-fry garlic and shallot 1 minute. Add chicken, coriander, soy sauce and pepper and stir-fry 2 or 3 minutes or until chicken is lightly browned. Remove from heat and stir in chopped cilantro.

Mix together bean sprouts, grated carrot and cilantro leaves. Place on serving plates and top with warm chicken mixture. Arrange nectarine and banana slices around edge of each salad and serve immediately.

Makes 4 servings.

Total Cals: 1018   Total fat: 25.6 g
Cals per portion: 254   Fat per portion: 6.4 g

——— EIGHT-TREASURE SALAD ———

12 oz. lean cooked skinless turkey
1 red, 1 green and 1 yellow bell pepper
4 oz. snow peas
2 oz. oyster mushrooms
1 bunch green onions
2 teaspoons sesame oil
1 tablespoon white rice vinegar
1 teaspoon honey
Freshly ground pepper
1/3 cup salted cashew nuts, crushed, to garnish

Cut turkey into 1/4-inch slices and arrange in center of 4 serving plates.

Halve and seed bell peppers. Cut into thin slices and arrange around turkey. Diagonally slice snow peas. Shred oyster mushrooms and green onions. Arrange on serving plates.

Mix together oil, vinegar, honey and pepper. Pour dressing over each salad, garnish with cashew nuts and serve.

Makes 4 servings.

Total Cals: 864   Total fat: 30.8 g
Cals per portion: 216   Fat per portion: 7.7 g

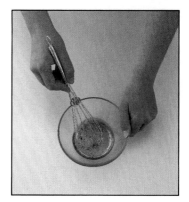

——BEEF & ORANGE SALAD——

1 tablespoon peanut oil
4 lean beef fillets, each weighing 4 oz., trimmed
3 tablespoons dark soy sauce
3 tablespoons dry sherry
1 teaspoon ground cinnamon
1 tablespoon brown sugar
Freshly ground pepper
6 oz. fresh young spinach leaves
1 (4-oz.) can water chestnuts, rinsed and sliced
4 oz. green onions, shredded
2 oranges, peeled and segmented
Strips of orange zest, to garnish

Heat oil in a nonstick or well-seasoned wok and fry beef steaks 2 minutes on each side. Drain on paper towels and wipe out wok. Mix together soy sauce, dry sherry, cinnamon, brown sugar and pepper. Return steaks to the wok, add water chestnuts and add soy sauce mixture. Bring to a boil, reduce heat and simmer 5 or 6 minutes, turning steaks halfway through.

Arrange spinach leaves on serving plates and top each with a steak, water chestnuts and sauce. Sprinkle with green onions and top with orange segments. Garnish with strips of orange zest and serve immediately.

Makes 4 servings.

Total Cals: 999   Total fat: 64.8 g
Cals per portion: 250   Fat per portion: 16.2 g

HOISIN BEEF SALAD

12 oz. lean roast beef, thinly sliced
1/2 head napa cabbage
2 large carrots
8 oz. daikon
1/4 cup chopped fresh chives
2 tablespoons hoisin sauce
1 teaspoon brown sugar
1 tablespoon red rice vinegar
1 teaspoon sesame oil
Carrot and daikon flowers, to garnish

Trim any fat from beef slices and cut into
1/2-inch strips.

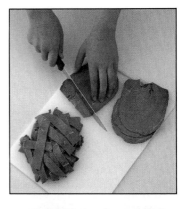

Discard damaged outer layer of cabbage
leaves and cut out center core. Shred leaves
finely and arrange on 4 serving plates. Peel
and grate the carrot and daikon and arrange
on top of the napa cabbage.

Arrange beef strips in the center and sprinkle
each plate with chives. In a small bowl, mix
together hoisin sauce, sugar, vinegar and oil
and drizzle over beef. Garnish with carrot
and daikon flowers and serve.

Makes 4 servings.

Total Cals: 766   Total fat: 21.6 g
Cals per portion: 191   Fat per portion: 5.4 g

—SWEET & SOUR FISH SALAD—

8 oz. trout fillets
8 oz. cod fillets
1-1/4 cups Chinese Vegetable Stock, page 14
2 tablespoons dry sherry
2 shallots, sliced
2 pineapple slices, chopped
1 small red bell pepper, diced
1 bunch of watercress
2 teaspoons sunflower oil
1 tablespoon red rice vinegar
Pinch of chile powder
1 teaspoon honey
Salt and freshly ground pepper
Pineapple pieces and watercress leaves, to garnish

Rinse and pat dry the fillets and place in a nonstick or well-seasoned wok. Add stock and dry sherry. Bring to a boil and simmer 7 or 8 minutes or until fish just begins to flake. Leave to cool in cooking liquor. Drain, remove skin and flake flesh into a bowl.

Carefully mix flaked fish with shallots, pineapple and bell pepper. Arrange watercress on 4 serving plates and top with fish mixture. Mix together oil, vinegar, chile powder, honey, salt and pepper and pour over salad. Garnish with pineapple pieces and watercress leaves and serve.

Makes 4 servings.

Total Cals: 605
Cals per portion: 151

Total fat: 19.4 g
Fat per portion: 4.85 g

— SZECHUAN SHRIMP SALAD —

1 teaspoon chile oil
1 teaspoon Szechuan peppercorns, toasted and
    ground
Pinch of salt
1 tablespoon white rice vinegar
1 teaspoon sugar
12 oz. cooked, peeled large shrimp, thawed and
    dried, if frozen
1/2 large cucumber
1 tablespoon sesame seeds
1/2 head napa cabbage, shredded
Fresh red chile strips and lemon wedges, to garnish

In a large bowl, mix together oil, peppercorns, salt, vinegar and sugar.

Add shrimp and mix well. Cover and chill
30 minutes. Thinly slice cucumber and slice
each piece into thin strips. Pat dry with
paper towels and mix into shrimp with
sesame seeds.

Arrange napa cabbage on 4 serving plates
and top with the shrimp mixture. Garnish
with chile strips and lemon wedges and
serve immediately.

Makes 4 servings.

Total Cals: 550   Total fat: 17.9 g
Cals per portion: 137   Fat per portion: 4.5 g

—SUMMER NOODLE SALAD—

6 oz. egg noodles
1 teaspoon sesame oil
2 tablespoons crunchy peanut butter
2 tablespoons light soy sauce
2 teaspoons sugar
Pinch of chile powder
1 lb. tomatoes, thinly sliced
1 bunch green onions, finely chopped
4 oz. bean sprouts
1 large carrot, grated
8 pitted dates, finely chopped

Cook noodles in boiling water 4 or 5 minutes or until tender but firm to the bite. Drain well and rinse in cold water. Leave in cold water until required.

Mix together oil, peanut butter, soy sauce, sugar and chile powder. Drain noodles well, place in a large bowl and mix in peanut sauce. Arrange tomato slices on a serving plate.

Using chopsticks or 2 forks, toss the green onions, bean sprouts, grated carrot and dates into the noodles and mix well. Pile on top of the sliced tomato and serve.

Makes 4 servings.

Total Cals: 1241   Total fat: 33.3 g
Cals per portion: 310   Fat per portion: 8.3 g

TOFU SALAD

12 oz. tofu, drained and rinsed
2 tablespoons dark soy sauce
2 tablespoons rice wine
4 oz. snow peas
4 oz. baby corn
2 small red bell peppers, quartered
2 tablespoons ground almonds
2 garlic cloves, finely chopped
2 tablespoons cornstarch
Salt and freshly ground pepper
1 tablespoon sunflower oil
2 tablespoons chopped fresh chives, to garnish

Cut tofu into 1/2-inch cubes and place on a plate. Spoon over soy sauce and wine. Cover and chill 1 hour.

Bring a saucepan of water to a boil. Add snow peas, baby corn and bell peppers and cook 2 minutes. Drain well and rinse in cold water. Leave in cold water until required. Remove tofu from soy sauce mixture and drain well. On a plate, mix together almonds, garlic, cornstarch, salt and pepper. Toss tofu in almond mixture.

Heat oil in a nonstick or well-seasoned wok and stir-fry tofu 4 or 5 minutes or until golden. Drain well on paper towels. Drain vegetables and arrange on serving plates. Top with tofu, garnish with chives and serve.

Makes 4 servings.

Total Cals: 925
Cals per portion: 231

Total fat: 54.2 g
Fat per portion: 13.55 g

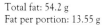

– SESAME GARLIC VEGETABLES –

8 oz. broccoli
1 large green bell pepper
2 small zucchini
8 oz. asparagus
2 garlic cloves, thinly sliced
2 teaspoons sesame oil
1 tablespoon sesame seeds

Slice broccoli into small flowerets. Slice zucchini into 1-inch pieces and halve. Cut bell pepper into 8. Trim away tough ends from asparagus and slice into 2-inch pieces. Place vegetables in a colander and rinse well.

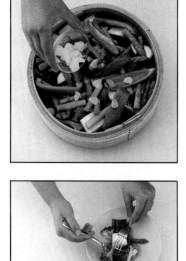

Bring a wok or large saucepan of water to a boil. Arrange vegetables on a layer of parchment paper in a steamer and place over water. Sprinkle with garlic and sesame oil. Cover and steam 10 minutes.

Remove vegetables from steamer and place on warmed serving plates. Sprinkle with sesame seeds and serve with soy sauce, for dipping. Ideal accompaniment for Five-Spice Salmon Steaks, page 41.

Makes 4 servings.

Total Cals: 346
Cals per portion: 86

Total fat: 20.6 g
Fat per portion: 5.15 g

RED-ROAST VEGETABLES

1 lb. sweet potatoes
12 oz. turnips
3 large carrots
1 tablespoon sunflower oil
2 fresh red chiles, seeded and chopped
1 garlic clove, finely chopped
1/2-inch piece fresh ginger root, peeled and finely
    chopped
2 tablespoons hoisin sauce
1/4 cup dark soy sauce
6 tablespoons Chinese Vegetable Stock, page 14
Strips of fresh ginger root, to garnish

Cut sweet potato into pieces 2 inches long and 1/2-inch wide. Cut turnips and carrots into 1-inch pieces.

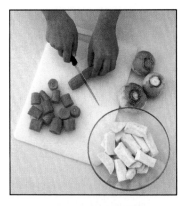

Preheat oven to 400F (205C). Bring a large saucepan of water to a boil, add vegetables and cook 5 minutes. Drain well. Place drained vegetables in a nonstick roasting pan.

In a small bowl, mix together remaining ingredients except garnish and spoon over vegetables. Stir thoroughly to coat vegetables and roast 30 minutes, basting occasionally, until tender. Garnish with strips of ginger and serve. Ideal accompaniment to roast meats such as Roast Pork with Honey, page 85.

Makes 4 servings.

Total Cals: 811   Total fat: 18.7 g
Cals per portion: 203   Fat per portion: 4.7 g

— SPICY STIR-FRIED CABBAGE —

1 lb. bok choy
1/2 head napa cabbage
1 tablespoon peanut oil
2 garlic cloves, finely chopped
1 tablespoon light soy sauce
1 teaspoon five-spice powder
1 teaspoon chile sauce
Salt and freshly ground pepper
Sliced fresh red chile, to garnish

Discard damaged outer leaves from bok choy
and cabbage. Break bok choy leaves from
stem, rinse well and dry on paper towels.
Discard coarse stem at base of leaves then
shred finely.

Bring a large saucepan of water to a boil and
cook the bok choy for a few seconds until
just wilted. Drain well and rinse in cold
water. Drain thoroughly and pat dry with
paper towels. Remove core from napa
cabbage, and shred finely.

Heat oil in a nonstick or well-seasoned wok
and stir-fry bok choy and garlic 2 minutes.
Add the napa cabbage and all the remaining
ingredients except the garnish and stir-fry
2 minutes. Garnish with sliced red chile and
serve immediately. Ideal accompaniment for
Beef with Oyster Sauce, page 80.

Makes 4 servings.

Total Cals: 274   Total fat: 18.1 g
Cals per portion: 68   Fat per portion: 4.5 g

GARLIC EGGPLANT

1 lb. eggplant
1/4 cup salt
1 tablespoon sunflower oil
2 garlic cloves, thinly sliced
3 tablespoons dark soy sauce
5 tablespoons rice wine
1 tablespoon yellow bean sauce
Freshly ground pepper
4 green onions, finely chopped
Shredded and sliced green onions, to garnish

Halve eggplant lengthwise. Halve again and cut into 1/2-inch thick pieces.

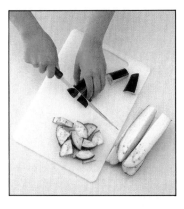

Layer eggplant in a bowl with the salt and leave for 30 minutes. Rinse well and dry on paper towels. Heat the oil in a nonstick or well-seasoned wok and stir-fry eggplant and garlic 2 or 3 minutes or until lightly browned.

Add all remaining ingredients except green onions. Bring to a boil, reduce heat and simmer 5 minutes or until softened. Stir in chopped green onions, garnish with shredded and sliced green onions and serve. Ideal accompaniment for Stir-fried Sesame Lamb, page 89.

Makes 4 servings.

Total Cals: 363   Total fat: 16.7 g
Cals per portion: 91   Fat per portion: 4.2 g

CHILE ROAST PEPPERS

1 large red bell pepper
1 large orange bell pepper
1 large green bell pepper
1 large yellow bell pepper
1 tablespoon dark soy sauce
1 teaspoon chile sauce
1 tablespoon sunflower oil
Freshly ground pepper
2 tablespoons chopped fresh chives

Halve bell peppers lengthwise, remove core and seeds then halve again. Place in a nonstick roasting pan.

Preheat oven to 375F (190C). In a small bowl, mix together the remaining ingredients except the chives and spoon over the bell peppers, turning to make sure they are well coated. Roast 30 minutes, basting occasionally, or until softened.

Transfer roast bell peppers to warmed serving plates, sprinkle with chives and serve. Ideal accompaniment for Ginger Chicken Patties, page 51.

Makes 4 servings.

Total Cals: 339   Total fat: 16.7 g
Cals per portion: 85   Fat per portion: 4.2 g

— PAN-COOKED VEGETABLES —

1 oz. dried Chinese mushrooms, soaked in hot water
   20 minutes
1 tablespoon peanut oil
1 whole cinnamon stick, broken
4 oz. shallots, quartered
8 oz. baby corn
4 oz. small broccoli flowerets
2 tablespoons dark soy sauce
1/4 cup dry sherry
1 tablespoon brown sugar
4 oz. snow peas
1 (4-oz.) can water chestnuts, rinsed
1 (4-oz.) can bamboo shoots, drained and sliced
Salt and freshly ground pepper

Drain mushrooms and squeeze out any excess water. Discard stems and thinly slice caps. Heat oil in a nonstick or well-seasoned wok and stir-fry the mushrooms, cinnamon, shallots, baby corn and broccoli 2 or 3 minutes until lightly browned.

Add soy sauce, sherry and sugar and bring to a boil. Reduce heat and simmer 5 minutes. Add remaining ingredients, mix well and cook 3 minutes. Discard cinnamon and serve with noodles.

Makes 4 servings.

Total Cals: 559   Total fat: 17.9 g
Cals per portion: 140   Fat per portion: 4.5 g

GREEN RICE

1-1/4 cups long-grain white rice, rinsed
3-1/2 cups Chinese Vegetable Stock, page 14
8 oz. small broccoli flowerets
8 oz. fresh spinach, tough ribs removed
1 tablespoon peanut oil
2 garlic cloves, finely chopped
1 fresh green chile, seeded and chopped
1 bunch green onions, finely chopped
1 (8-oz.) package frozen green peas
2 tablespoons light soy sauce
Salt and freshly ground pepper
1/4 cup chopped fresh chives
Fresh chives, to garnish

Place rice and stock in a large saucepan, bring to a boil, reduce heat and simmer 25 minutes or until rice is cooked and liquid has been absorbed. Cook broccoli in a saucepan of boiling water 2 minutes. Drain and set aside. Blanch spinach in a saucepan of boiling water a few seconds or until just wilted. Drain well, shred and set aside.

Heat oil in a nonstick or well-seasoned wok and stir-fry garlic, chile, green onions and broccoli 1 minute. Add cooked rice, spinach, frozen peas and soy sauce. Season with salt and pepper and simmer 5 minutes. Stir in chopped chives. Garnish with chives and serve with a mixed salad.

Makes 4 servings.

Total Cals: 1599
Cals per portion: 400

Total fat: 24.1 g
Fat per portion: 6.02 g

-BEAN & MUSHROOM NOODLES-

6 oz. black-eyed peas
6 oz. vermicelli rice noodles
1 tablespoon sunflower oil
2 garlic cloves, finely chopped
2 shallots, finely chopped
2 teaspoons fermented black beans
1 oz. dried Chinese mushrooms, soaked in hot water
   20 minutes, drained and caps sliced
4 oz. button mushrooms, sliced
4 oz. oyster mushrooms, sliced
3 tablespoons light soy sauce
Salt and freshly ground pepper
1/4 cup chopped fresh chives

Place peas in a saucepan, add enough water to cover and bring to a boil. Cover and simmer 45 minutes or until just softened. Drain and rinse in cold water. Bring a large saucepan of water to a boil. Turn off heat and add noodles. Loosen with chopsticks or 2 forks and leave to soak 3 minutes. Drain well and rinse in cold water.

Heat oil in a nonstick or well-seasoned wok and stir-fry garlic, shallots, black beans and mushrooms 2 or 3 minutes. Add black-eyed peas and stir-fry 1 minute. Add soy sauce, salt, pepper and noodles, mix well and simmer 2 or 3 minutes to warm through. Stir in chives, transfer to serving plates and serve with a salad.

Makes 4 servings.

Total Cals: 1535   Total fat: 29.5 g
Cals per portion: 384   Fat per portion: 7.4 g

— NOODLES WITH CHOP SUEY —

1 tablespoon peanut oil
2 garlic cloves, finely chopped
1 green bell pepper, thinly sliced
1 red bell pepper, thinly sliced
8 oz. shallots, chopped
2 small zucchini, cut into matchstick strips
2 large carrots, cut into matchstick strips
4 oz. bean sprouts
2 teaspoons sugar
2 tablespoons light soy sauce
1/4 cup Chinese Vegetable Stock, page 14
Salt and freshly ground pepper
8 oz. egg noodles

Heat the oil in a nonstick or well-seasoned wok and stir-fry garlic, green and red bell peppers, shallots, zucchini and carrots 2 or 3 minutes or until just softened. Add all remaining ingredients except noodles, bring to a boil, reduce heat and simmer 6 or 7 minutes.

Meanwhile, bring a large saucepan of water to a boil, add noodles and cook 5 minutes or until just tender. Drain well and transfer to warmed serving plates. Top with the vegetable mixture and serve.

Makes 4 servings.

Total Cals: 1354	Total fat: 37 g
Cals per portion: 338	Fat per portion: 9.25 g

——— STEAMED DIM SUM ———

4 oz. tofu, drained and mashed
2 green onions, finely chopped
1 stalk celery, finely chopped
1 tablespoon chopped fresh cilantro
1/2-inch piece fresh ginger root, peeled and finely
   chopped
2 teaspoons light soy sauce
Salt and freshly ground pepper
16 wonton skins
Cilantro leaves, to garnish

Put all ingredients except wonton skins and garnish into a bowl and mix together until well combined. Spoon a portion onto each wonton skin.

Dampen wonton skins with water. Bring up sides of each wonton, pressing them around filling and leaving tops open. Flatten the bottoms.

Bring a wok or large saucepan of water to a boil. Place wontons on a sheet of parchment paper in a steamer and place over the water. Cover and steam 15 minutes. Garnish with cilantro and serve on a bed of rice, with chile sauce as a dip.

Makes 4 servings.

Total Cals: 468   Total fat: 12.3 g
Cals per portion: 117   Fat per portion: 3.1 g

SZECHUAN PANCAKES

2 cups all-purpose flour
2 teaspoons sesame oil
Strips of fresh green and red chile and celery leaves,
  to garnish
FILLING:
2 tablespoons cornstarch
1 teaspoon Szechuan peppercorns, toasted and
  ground
Large pinch of salt
8 oz. tofu, drained and cut into 3/4-inch cubes
1 tablespoon sunflower oil
2 garlic cloves, finely chopped
2 tablespoons light soy sauce
6 oz. vegetable chow-chow, shredded

Sift flour into a bowl and, using chopsticks
or a fork, mix in 2/3 cup boiling water, to
form a firm dough. Knead on a lightly
floured surface until smooth. Divide dough
into 8 and roll out each portion to form a
6-inch diameter pancake. Heat a nonstick
skillet. Lightly brush pancakes on each side
with oil and cook 1 or 2 minutes on each
side. Drain on paper towels, layer between
sheets of parchment paper and keep warm.

Place cornstarch, peppercorns and salt on a
plate and toss tofu in the mixture until well
coated. Heat oil in a nonstick or well-
seasoned wok and stir-fry tofu and garlic 2 or
3 minutes or until browned. Add soy sauce
and vegetable chow-chow and stir-fry 3
minutes. Place a little tofu mixture on each
pancake and fold pancake around the filling.
Garnish and serve.

Makes 4 servings.

Total Cals: 1394   Total fat: 38.3 g
Cals per portion: 348   Fat per portion: 9.6 g

TOFU & PEPPERS

8 oz. fresh tofu, drained and cut into 3/4-inch cubes
1 tablespoon dark soy sauce
1 tablespoon sweet sherry
1-inch piece fresh ginger root, peeled and finely
  chopped
Salt and freshly ground pepper
1 tablespoon sunflower oil
1 fresh red chile, seeded and finely chopped
2 garlic cloves, thinly sliced
1 red bell pepper, thinly sliced
1 green bell pepper, thinly sliced
1 yellow bell pepper, thinly sliced
3 tablespoons chopped fresh basil

Place tofu on a plate or in a shallow dish.
Mix together soy sauce, sherry, ginger, salt
and pepper. Spoon over tofu, cover and chill
30 minutes.

Heat oil in a nonstick or well-seasoned wok
and stir-fry tofu mixture, chile and garlic
2 minutes. Add bell peppers and stir-fry 4
minutes. Stir in basil and serve immediately
with noodles.

Makes 4 servings.

Total Cals: 423   Total fat: 25.5 g
Cals per portion: 106   Fat per portion: 6.4 g

——GREEN TEA FRUIT SALAD——

4 teaspoons jasmine tea leaves
2 tablespoons dry sherry
2 tablespoons sugar
1 lime
2 kiwi fruit
8 oz. fresh lychees
1/4 honeydew melon
4 oz. seedless green grapes
Lime slices, to decorate

Place tea leaves in a small bowl and add 1-1/4 cups boiling water. Leave to steep 5 minutes. Strain through a strainer into a saucepan.

Stir in sherry and sugar. Using a vegetable peeler, pare the zest from lime and add to pan. Squeeze juice from the lime and add juice to pan. Bring to a boil, reduce heat and simmer 5 minutes. Leave to cool, then discard lime zest.

Peel and thinly slice kiwi fruit. Peel, halve and pit lychees. Peel melon and slice thinly. Arrange prepared fruits and grapes in small clusters on serving plates. Spoon cooled tea syrup over fruit, decorate and serve.

Makes 4 servings.

Total Cals: 401   Total fat: 1.2 g
Cals per portion: 100   Fat per portion: 0.3 g

—CARAMEL SESAME BANANAS—

4 bananas
Juice of 1 lemon
4 oz. sugar
2 tablespoons sesame seeds
Mint sprigs and lemon slices, to decorate

Peel bananas and cut into 2-inch pieces. Place in a bowl, add lemon juice and stir to coat.

Place sugar and 1/4 cup water in a saucepan and heat gently, stirring, until the sugar dissolves. Bring to a boil and cook 5 or 6 minutes or until the mixture caramelizes and turns golden brown. Drain bananas well and arrange on parchment paper.

Drizzle caramel over the bananas, working quickly as the caramel sets within a few seconds. Sprinkle with sesame seeds. Allow to cool 5 minutes, then carefully peel away from paper, decorate and serve.

Makes 4 servings.

Total Cals: 937   Total fat: 13.5 g
Cals per portion: 234   Fat per portion: 3.4 g

Note: Tossing the banana in lemon juice prevents it from turning brown.

—LYCHEE & GINGER MOUSSE—

12 oz. fresh lychees, peeled and pitted
1/2 teaspoon ground ginger
3 tablespoons sweet sherry
2 pieces stem ginger in syrup, chopped
1 oz. ground almonds
2 teaspoons plain gelatin powder dissolved in 2
   tablespoons boiling water
2 egg whites
Sliced stem ginger and mint leaves, to decorate

Place lychees in a food processor with the
ground ginger, sherry and chopped ginger.
Blend until smooth. Transfer to a small bowl
and stir in ground almonds and gelatin
mixture.

Chill 30 or 40 minutes or until beginning to
set. In a large, grease-free bowl, whisk egg
whites until very stiff. Using a large metal
spoon, carefully fold in the lychee mixture.

Divide mixture among 4 sundae glasses or
dishes and chill 1 hour or until set. Decorate
with stem ginger and mint leaves and serve.

Makes 4 servings.

Total Cals: 479   Total fat: 16.2 g
Cals per portion: 120   Fat per portion: 4.05 g

— FRUIT-FILLED WHITE CREPES —

3 egg whites, lightly beaten
1/4 cup cornstarch
1 teaspoon sunflower oil
Mint sprigs, to decorate
FILLING:
4 slices fresh pineapple, chopped
2 kiwi fruit, peeled and quartered
1/2 mango, peeled, pitted and sliced
1/2 papaya, peeled, seeded and chopped
2 tablespoons dry sherry
1 tablespoon brown sugar
1 whole cinnamon stick, broken
2 star anise

Place all the filling ingredients in a nonstick or well-seasoned wok and mix gently. Bring to a boil, reduce heat and simmer very gently 10 minutes. Remove and discard cinnamon stick and star anise. Set aside. Meanwhile, make the crepes. Put egg whites and cornstarch in a bowl and stir in 8 teaspoons water, mixing well to form a smooth paste.

Brush a nonstick or well-seasoned crepe pan with a little oil and heat. Pour in a quarter of the mixture, tilting pan to cover the bottom. Cook 1 minute on one side only, until set. Drain on paper towels, layer with parchment paper and keep warm while making the remaining 3 crepes. Lay crepes cooked-side up, fill with the fruit and fold crepes over the filling. Decorate and serve.

Makes 4 servings.

Total Cals: 674   Total fat: 5.7 g
Cals per portion: 168   Fat per portion: 1.4 g

—— STUFFED RAMBUTANS ——

1 small banana, chopped
Grated zest and juice of 1 lime
16 rambutans
12 pitted dates, chopped
1 papaya, peeled, seeded and chopped
Strips of lime zest, to decorate

Mix banana with lime zest and juice and set aside. Slice top off rambutans, exposing tip of the pit. Using a sharp, small-bladed knife, carefully slice down around the pit, loosening flesh away from pit.

Peel away skin, and slice lengthwise through flesh at quarterly intervals. Gently pull down the flesh to expose pit and carefully cut away pit. The flesh should now resemble a four-petalled flower.

In a food processor or blender, blend banana and dates until smooth. Place a teaspoon of filling in the center of each rambutan and bring up the sides to enclose filling. Cover and chill 30 minutes. Blend papaya in a food processor or blender until smooth, pass through a strainer and spoon onto four serving plates. Top with rambutans, decorate with strips of lime zest and serve.

Makes 4 servings.

Total Cals: 537
Cals per portion: 134

Total fat: 1.4 g
Fat per portion: 0.35 g

—STEAMED FRUIT DUMPLINGS—

1 small banana, chopped
Grated zest and juice of 1 small lemon
1 oz. dried mango or dried apricots, chopped
8 pitted dates, chopped
1 oz. ground almonds
Large pinch ground cinnamon
12 round wonton skins
1 egg white, lightly beaten
2 teaspoons powdered sugar
Strips of dried mango and date and mint sprigs, to
    decorate

Place banana, lemon zest and juice, mango, dates, almonds and cinnamon in a food processor and blend until smooth.

Divide fruit mixture among wonton skins, placing it in the center of each one. Brush edges of the wonton skins with egg white, fold in half to form crescent shapes and press edges together to seal.

Bring a wok or large saucepan of water to a boil. Place dumplings on a sheet of parchment paper in a steamer and place over the water. Cover and steam 10 minutes or until soft. Dust with powdered sugar, decorate and serve.

Makes 4 servings.

Total Cals: 777   Total fat: 21.9 g
Cals per portion: 194   Fat per portion: 5.5 g

INDEX